The Economics of Health Professional Education and Careers

A WORLD BANK STUDY

The Economics of Health Professional Education and Careers

Insights from a Literature Review

Barbara McPake, Allison Squires, Agya Mahat, and Edson C. Araujo

WORLD BANK GROUP

Contents

Boxes

Figures

Tables

Acknowledgments

The publication greatly benefited from comments received from Christopher Herbst (Health Specialist, HNP Global Practice, World Bank Group) and Francisco Marmolejo (Lead Education Specialist, Education Global Practice, World Bank Group) and thorough editing by Jonathan Aspin. The authors would like to thank Meriel "Molly" McCollum (New York University College of Nursing) and Mimi Niles (New York University College of Nursing) for their editorial and reference management contributions to this report.

This publication was supported by a generous grant provided by the Norwegian Ministry of Foreign Affairs and the Norwegian Agency for Development Cooperation (NORAD) through the Multi-Donor Trust Fund Strengthening Human Resources for Health Policy in Developing Countries.

Acknowledgments

Executive Summary

The formation of health professionals is critical for the health system to function and to achieve its universal health coverage (UHC) goals, and this is well recognized by the majority of governments that plan to ensure enough training places and aim to regulate in order to ensure quality. But the importance of market forces is often overlooked, resulting in interventions and regulations that often fail to achieve their intended effects.

The purpose of this study is to inform the design of health professionals' education policies to better manage health labor market forces toward UHC. It documents what is known about the influence of market forces on the health-professional formation process. It aims to cover all types of health professional (although the constraints of the literature resulted in a primary focus on physicians and nurses). While it aims at a long-term perspective, available evidence covers mainly the last two decades. The report sought to answer the following questions:

- What have been the large global and regional trends in the development of health professions?
- How have these trends affected the career decisions of current and potential health professionals?
- What is the evidence base on the value and effectiveness of health professional education of different types?
- How has the market for health professional education evolved, and with what interrelationships with the health labor and health care markets?

The contexts of the market for health professional training have been subject to important changes in recent decades, in particular the growing extent of employment of mid-level cadres of health professionals; changes in technology and the associated growth of high-skilled occupations; the increasing interconnectedness of national health systems through globalization, with its implications for international health professional mobility; and the greater complexity of the public–private mix in employment options.

The first has involved the creation of new training opportunities, the value of which is suggested by a fairly convincing body of evidence that such new cadres are contributing significantly to the provision of effective health care for underserved populations or of services in short supply. The expansion of the role of mid-level cadres has been accompanied by a growing role also for "low-level" providers, something particularly pronounced in low- and middle-income countries (LMICs) in the form of community health workers but also present in high-income countries in roles such as care assistants.

Technological changes in the health care sector have resulted in substantial increases in returns to high-skilled occupations, boosting the demand for specialization training and resulting in a skill-biased composition of the health workforce. Globalization has increased international migration of health professionals, which reached unprecedented levels in the early years of the twenty-first century. There has also been a growing trend toward considering the needs of the global health market when setting training curricula, which has made some curricula less appropriate for preparing staff for their own countries or regions. This demand for training in internationally tradable health professional skills also partially explains the growth of a private for-profit health professional training industry (particularly marked in some LMICs).

The market for health professional training and its outcomes is skewed by market failures inherent to health care, transmitted through a series of derived markets. Most importantly, the wage rate fails to reflect the value of health professional work as judged by its social returns (contribution to public health) because of the following:

- Information problems in the health care market create a gap between willingness to pay and informed willingness to pay (for the most effective interventions).
- The distribution of ability to pay causes those with high public health need to have weak demand.
- Government efforts to replace individual willingness to pay with public finance are affected by a combination of weak fiscal capacity, weak governance, and/or weak political will to direct public investment to the poorest and least healthy in the most cost-effective way.

There is evidence that the wage rate is an important influence over the choices made by health professionals among educational and training opportunities. It also further influences the status and prestige attached to different health professions which have their own independent influence on those choices. Training schools reflect those dual pressures, with organizational and cultural influences reinforcing trends toward ever greater specialization and movement from primary care, particularly for the medical profession but also for other health professionals. These trends undermine health systems' compatibility with UHC goals.

These pressures are increasing over time in most parts of the world. Evidence of the tendencies of health professionals to seek to specialize and subspecialize and to choose careers other than those in primary care and serving remote and disadvantaged populations is consistent across the high-, middle-, and low-income countries, across health professional cadres, and is consistently increasing over time with only a few exceptions. A range of sources suggest that there is a significantly higher rate of return to more specialized education and that the ratio of the rate of return to specialized over general medical education has been increasing over time. Explanations include the influence of technology, which may ensure that certain specialist roles are associated with increasing productivity, and the greater role of specialist than generalist physicians in institutionalized price setting processes, for example in setting reimbursement levels of major insurers. Evidence of financial returns to specialist nurse training suggests a much more mixed picture, with some types of advanced training evaluated as having negative returns.

Nevertheless, there is a growing body of evidence that "lifestyle factors" such as workload, working hours, and stress-related factors are playing an increasing role in influencing the choices of health professional students in high-income countries. These are less detrimental to the prospects of primary care, which is at least usually ranked in an intermediate position in relation to lifestyle, although this varies from one country to another. This influence does not yet seem to have been sufficient to reverse trends in the popularity of specialization compared to generalism, but offers some grounds for optimism with respect to longer-term trends. Lifestyle factors do not appear important in the choices of students in LMICs, however.

The high international return to health professional skills in part explains fast-emerging markets for private for-profit training opportunities, although in a fast-growing middle-income country such as India this phenomenon is equally explained by the return to such skills promised by the emerging middle class. Evidence of the emergence of these markets for medicine in India and for nursing in Nepal suggests difficulties of regulation and concomitant risks of quality diminution which may also contaminate quality levels in the public sector.

The marked differences in return to medical specialization relative to medical generalism and primary care and to serving the rural, remote, and disadvantaged relative to the urban elite for all health professionals exemplify the conflict between health labor market forces and stated policy intentions. Increasing the income levels of generalists, primary care providers, and those serving rural, remote, and disadvantaged populations is constrained by sustainability and affordability issues and, in many cases, by an absence of political will. It may be easier to improve returns to the choice to train for socially valued roles by allocating training subsidies accordingly. Community-based and -focused training schools have demonstrated their greater capacity to produce health professionals for socially valued roles in a diverse range of settings. This understanding should also influence the distribution of public subsidy to a greater extent than is usually the case.

There is a need to ensure that market forces align with the intentions of planning and regulation and the needs of UHC and that health labor market analysis can provide support in designing policies that help to achieve this.

Policy Recommendations

- Recognize the importance of market forces in developing health professional formation policies
- Prioritize investment in training mid- and low-level providers for which there is good evidence of high social rate of return
- Regulate training curricula to balance pressures to provide training for international markets and ensure focus on producing professionals capable of meeting local needs
- Mobilize private international investment in systems for regulating private training providers; companies that profit from medical tourism having a strong stake in achieving better regulation
- Balance professional representation with public representation in key policy and regulatory bodies that influence the rate of return to specialization within all health professions, given that the role of public representatives is to offset the bias toward specialists among professional representatives
- Prioritize and weight subsidies in nursing and medical training toward generalist training; high private rates of return to specialist training implying that those benefiting will be willing to invest in their own training more
- Invest in expanding rural and community-based health professional training settings
- Encourage innovation in health professional formation processes, considering opportunities both for new technologies and for better understanding and exploitation of scale efficiencies.

Abbreviations

CHW	community health worker
GDP	gross domestic product
GP	general practitioner
HIC	high-income country
HRH	human resources for health
LMIC	low- and middle-income countries
NPV	net present values
RORE	rates of return to education
RUC	Relative Value Scale Update Committee
SCPHN	specialist community public health nurses
UHC	universal health coverage
WHO	World Health Organization

CHAPTER 1

Introduction

The health sector is shaped by its professionals. The processes by which they are selected for training, trained, and then deployed are therefore critical for the functioning of any health system. Most governments recognize the importance of these processes and heavily subsidize training of health professionals and attempt to regulate the outcomes—numbers and types, and quality of training (McPake et al. 2013). However, these outcomes are also considerably influenced by market forces. For example, the demand for places in training schools reflects (among other things) the economic returns for the trainees of investing their time and in most cases money in the training course, thereby affecting students' choices among specialties.

Market forces are often more influential than government policies on health professionals' career choices. The best education is often perceived, by students, employers, and society more broadly, to be one that will teach providers the skills valued in the market, as opposed to those based on population needs. Technological changes in health care, for example, have had a profound influence in creating a movement toward higher skilled labor by increasing its rate of return. Similarly, specialties with high rates of return to educational invest-ment—resulting in monetary and lifestyle management gains—often draw the greatest interest from prospective students. The number of privately owned training schools is growing in many countries; they are run for profit and with behavior largely shaped by market forces. Commercial support for continuing medical education has also grown steadily over the past decade in many parts of the world. The consequent "medicalization" of life promotes a disease-oriented pattern of health professional education, de-emphasizing the wellness- and pre-vention-oriented approaches of primary care.

The market for health professional education is wide ranging, encompassing multiple types of health professionals with different lengths and depths of training, from community health workers to specialist physicians. And although here, too, market forces may exert greater influence on health professionals' education systems than planning and regulation, consideration of the effects of market forces seems to have had the less influence on shaping human resources for health (HRH) policies. The interaction between the education system (education market) and health system (health care markets) is mediated by the labor market for health workers. In ideal situations, the intersecting systems produce a balance between population health needs and health worker demand/supply. But labor markets seldom clear, that is, imbalances persist between these elements, seen notably in health worker undersupply (shortages), and under- and unemployment. These imbalances tend to result in the neglect of poor, remote, and rural populations, and of preventive and promotive care (figure 1.1 and box 1.1).

An understanding of how health labor markets respond to health care market signals and how these responses influence the dynamics of the health professionals' education market is, therefore, critical for the functioning of the health system and the achievement of universal health coverage (UHC) goals. The objective of this paper is to inform the design of policies to better manage health labor market forces by documenting what is known about the influence of market forces on the health professional formation process. It aims to address issues from a global perspective, seeking out patterns of difference between low-, middle-, and high-income countries and across regions of the world. It also aims to understand the evolution of the health professions and of health labor markets over the last 30 years, and to cover all types of health professional, although the constraints of the literature engendered a focus on physicians and nurses.

Figure 1.1 The Interaction between Education Systems, Labor Markets, and Health Systems

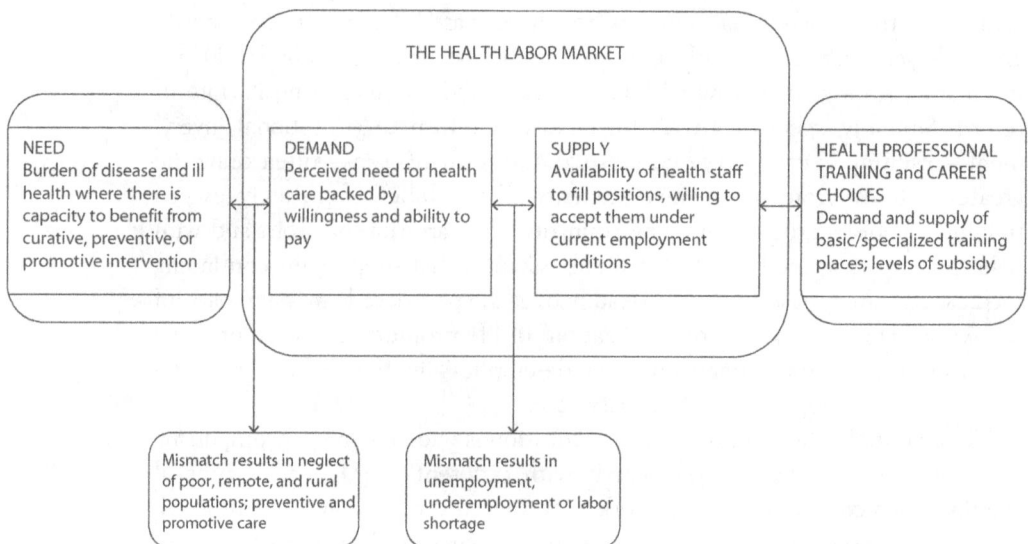

Source: World Bank.

Box 1.1   Market Failures in Health Worker Labor Markets

This study focuses on the market influences on the "formation" stages of a health profession-al's career considered as those stages that involve formal, accredited education. Of course, markets continue to shape access to appropriate and effective health professionals after those professionals have completed formal education and as they choose between alternative jobs in and outside the health sector. This wider labor market literature and its implications for human resources for health policies have been reviewed, with the following perspectives offered (McPake et al. 2014).

The most important variable in any labor market analysis is the wage rate. In health labor markets there are two critical wage-related considerations: market failures and public sector wage-setting processes imply that wages cannot be assumed to represent measures of productivity or of either demand- or need-based values of health professionals' work; and the tendency toward relative rigidity of wages in the public relative to the private sector.

These two considerations may account for a series of health labor market phenomena including rural–urban imbalance, internal and external migration, poor retention of health staff, dual practice, overall shortage of health professionals in public sectors, low productivity, and the prevalence of bonuses and allowances as significant components of public health professionals' pay.

From this perspective, rural–urban imbalance can be viewed as arising from a combination of insufficient private demand for care in rural areas relative to need, and insufficient compensating public demand. The rural population cannot afford to pay directly at a price level capable of attracting sufficient health professionals. And while the public sector aims to correct this insufficiency by taking over the payer role, wage rigidities, limited resources, and inadequate political will prevent health professionals' pay from reflecting the relative hardships of rural practice, including the limited opportunities for dual practice.

A similar analysis explains why low-income countries cannot compete with high-income countries, so health professionals are lost to migration; why the public sector cannot compete with the private sector, so health professionals are wholly or partly lost to the private sector; and low productivity, because health professionals do not end up in those jobs where their productivity would be highest. Recognition that rigidities (such as public sector pay comparability requirements between health and other sectors) are frustrating health sector policy intentions has often led to bonuses and allowances, which appear to have grown as a share of health professionals' pay in low-income countries over the past 20 years.

McPake et al. (2014) identified studies that sought to measure the size of these influences on rural job acceptance and retention and on internal and external migration. Many of these used the discrete choice analysis approach, which uses hypothetical scenarios to elicit values for attributes of jobs from health professionals. These studies not only confirm the importance of pay levels and differentials in health professionals' job choices but also emphasize that other variables (including opportunities for study, amenities such as housing provision, equipment, and facilities supporting a professional standard of work, and good management) are also important.

In order to achieve these objectives a scoping review of the literature was undertaken (appendix A), seeking evidence on the following questions:

- What have been the large global and regional trends in the development of health professions?
- How have these trends affected the career decisions of current and potential health professionals?
- What is the evidence base on the value and effectiveness of health professional education of different types?
- How has the market for health professional education evolved, and with what interrelationships with the health labor and health care markets?

An integrative review approach was adopted to synthesize the content from the literature cited in this report. Unlike systematic reviews, integrative reviews include all literature relevant to the topic of interest. Research critique addresses the thematic gaps in the literature and does not aim to evaluate methods or address study weaknesses. Databases for the searches included PubMed, CINAHL, and SCIELO. Table A.1 and table A.2 in appendix A identify the search terms used for this review. Articles published before 1990 were excluded along with selected opinion papers. Gray literature reports and articles published in English, Portuguese, and Spanish were included.

The search retrieved 1,334 sources, clearly irrelevant material was excluded. These articles were further reviewed for relevance, coded by health profession and geographic region, and categorized according to the questions we sought to answer. The final number of sources selected for the review was 206. These were chosen because they had strong methods, policy analyses and program evaluations or were strong evidence syntheses with solid arguments.

The evidence collected from the literature review to answer the four questions is discussed in chapters 2–5. Chapter 6 draws conclusions, including the policy implications of the existing evidence base and the areas where gaps suggest the need for further research.

CHAPTER 2

Historical Trends and Globalization

During the last decades of the twentieth century, new roles and occupations emerged within health systems to meet health care market demands for services. Professionalization was faster for nonphysician health professions because of social changes related to the acceptability of women in the workplace (among other factors).

As professions organized, their ability to access or sustain the political, social, and economic power associated with the profession increased (Abbott 1988). New diagnostic and therapeutic cadres, such as nurse practitioners, physician assistants, and associate clinicians, evolved to fill the health labor market gaps in primary care and created new career pathways (DeMaria et al. 2012). Allied health roles expanded to provide specialized services and their value became apparent as patient outcomes improved. For example, physical and occupational therapies can save health systems substantial costs because they can be provided in the home or on an outpatient basis, thus helping to reduce rehospitalizations and risks of complications (Agency for Healthcare Research and Quality 2014).

In health care, specialized knowledge about a disease or condition is often needed to produce the best outcomes (Kendall-Gallagher et al. 2011). Specialized practice in health care means the provider has done one of two things: focused their training on treating and managing a specific disease or condition (for instance, infectious diseases) or a specific population (for example, geriatrics); or taken an exam that certifies they possess specialized knowledge gained from working with patients with a certain disease or condition (such as critical care nursing). Specialization often leads to significant professional and socioeconomic gains for the individual (Perales 2013; Stange 2014). Advances in technology can also incentivize specialized practice by creating a new niche area of practice that only the professional can perform. This usually lasts until the technology becomes widely available and cost analyses demonstrate that other cadres can effectively provide the technology-based service with equivalent outcomes (Walker et al 2012; Stanback, Mbonye, and Bekiita 2007).

Specialized training is usually at the postgraduate level for health professionals and can be by diploma, fellowship, or university degree (masters or doctorate).

For physicians, a postgraduate degree or diploma is almost mandatory for professional growth. Because health professions such as dentistry and midwifery are specialized practice areas in themselves, a specialized postgraduate degree has less importance unless its holder is planning an academic career or pursuing a further specialized area, like orthodontics or maxillofacial surgery (in the case of dentists). Many countries have dual education programs that prepare nursing professionals as midwives in order to address population health needs (Riley et al. 2012), but graduates from these programs do not always practice as midwives. Physician assistants and registered nurses can choose to work in specialized areas without a postgraduate degree and their specialty is determined by their place of work. Postgraduate qualifications for some categories of mid-level providers are often limited.

The need for mid-level providers varies by country, and the cadre evolves to fill service gaps left by shortages of all kinds of health workers. In the United States, for example, both the nurse practitioner and physician assistant professions were originally created to strengthen the primary care workforce, but both cadres can choose and switch their specialty area of practice. By contrast, in Sub-Saharan Africa, mid-level providers work across primary care settings. They are often known as clinical officers (this term is used in Kenya, Malawi, and Tanzania, for example) (Mbindyo, Blaauw, and English 2013).

In parallel with mid-level providers, low-level workers have also been increasingly promoted (Fulton et al. 2011). In high-income countries (HICs), one example is the expansion of roles of unlicensed assistive personnel who function as patient care assistants to nurses and allied health professionals in hospital and long-term care settings. For low- and middle-income countries (LMICs), the expanded use of community health workers (CHWs) to improve access to care or to conduct health education is the most important example. Brazil and Ethiopia provide good examples of CHW programs (Gragnolati, Lindelow, and Couttolenc 2013; Medhanyie et al. 2012). In both cases, formally educated professionals have supervisory responsibilities added to their roles, and where legal systems are strong, such duties also include responsibility for any work left undone or of poor quality by the lower-skilled role. Professionals often react to this "risk" by not delegating the assigned tasks to these cadres, thus adding to their burden due to distrust issues (Maestad, Torsvik, and Aakvik 2010).

The emergence of new cadres has often been met by resistance from professionals who traditionally provide the same services. Sociologists describe these dynamics as the interplay between maintaining the power of the profession in their particular market sphere, the jurisdiction over what they view as the market, and reinforcing the system of professions within the local context to maintain the status quo (Freidson 1970; Larson 1977; Abbott 1988). Interprofessional education can help mediate some of this resistance: it involves joint education between three or more health professions and can increase efficiency in education (Interprofessional Education Collaborative 2011). The experiences help increase understanding of roles in the health care system (Frenk et al. 2010;

Dower, Moore, and Langelier 2013), but when income is threatened due to task sharing and role changes, this approach may not help.

The above changes occurred across the world in concert with changing epidemiological and demographic conditions, along with insurance and payment systems that have affected health system operations to varying degrees. Aging and growing levels of noncommunicable and chronic diseases are placing ever-increasing demands on health systems, while the patient experience has become a central focus of health system operations and organization. Private education has also increased exponentially across the world as a solution to health worker shortages and market opportunities, though it is often poorly regulated, leading to inadequately trained and prepared graduates (World Health Organization 2006).

Another hallmark of twenty-first-century health professions is global mobility, one that draws many people into them. Factors driving migration include war or conflict, ethnic or racial discrimination, dissatisfaction with job opportunities, other economic issues, and a desire to see new places or have new experiences. Governments may encourage migration as a national policy, implicitly or explicitly, because of the economic benefits of remittances (Sana 2008; Zárate 2008). For example, in many countries training as a health professional is associated with opportunities for migration, and sometimes, better wages and career advancement. As Internet use spread rapidly around the world in the late 1990s, access to these opportunities grew rapidly, which expanded as HICs faced domestic production shortages and sought to fill vacancies with international workers.

Most studies on health worker migration focus on push and pull factors, that is, those in the source country, such as low salaries, poor management, and poor working conditions (including personal safety in the workplace), and those in the destination country, such as more interesting work, far higher salaries, and opportunities to travel. Gender and social conditions are other factors in health worker migration. Robinson, Murrells, and Griffiths' (2008) results suggested that age, family factors, and the presence of children also affect migration decisions, acting as retention factors for some locations.

The globalization approach to analyzing migration and the effects on health labor markets incorporates state immigration policies as a potential regulatory factor (Bach 2007; Drevdahl and Dorcy 2007; Humphries, Brugha, and McGee 2008). The Philippines has the longest history of developing policies on sending health workers (especially nurses) abroad for work all around the world, starting in the early years of this century (Choy 2006). Former British colonies (India and many African countries) were the next largest sending regions in the LMIC world (Dicicco-Bloom 2004; Dovlo 2007). Migration of health workers from Latin America to Spain for nursing work is a common yet not well-documented phenomenon (Malvárez et al., 2008).

Increased international opportunities outside the home country can therefore have two major impacts: stimulate domestic production of health workers and directly affect health professional education by introducing a bias in their skills (toward those more marketable in the global health labor market). The latter impact's risk is its potential to cause shortages in some countries through emigration, as seen in the early part of the twenty-first century. Preventing this outcome was the basis of the World Health Organization (WHO) Global Code of Practice on the International Recruitment of Health Personnel.[1] Health professional education, therefore, has increasingly the dual role of meeting both domestic and international demand for health workers.

Note

1. http://www.who.int/hrh/migration/code/practice/en/, accessed February 22, 2015.

CHAPTER 3

Specialty Choice among Health Professionals and Its Health Labor Market Determinants

Specialization affects countries' abilities to provide universal health coverage (UHC) due to additional costs that specialized services add to a health system's budget. Many studies show that improved and more equitable population health outcomes are associated with the presence of more primary care providers, but this is not the case with specialist supply. Moreover, the cost of health care is reduced with more primary care providers providing health care services because of their impact on preventive medicine, early diagnosis and management of diseases, and reduction in unnecessary and inappropriate specialty care (Starfield et al. 2005; Starfield, Shi, and Macinko 2005). Maintaining the appropriate balance between generalists and specialists in the supply of labor to the health system is therefore important in terms of both costs and effectiveness. This balance is dependent on the choices prospective health workers make as they navigate the health professional education and health labor markets (figure 3.1).

Technological advances in the health care industry have created a bias toward high skills, shifting the career preference of health professionals toward such specialties. Schumacher (2002) observes stability in demand for high-skilled workers in the health care industry in the United States. He observes that highly skilled health care workers received relatively higher wage growth in the period when real wages for all workers increased. They also received a higher premium for their skills even in the period when real wages in the industry fell (Schumacher 2002). When institutions that employ health workers offer more favorable wage rates and working conditions to those with certain specialties, more graduates will prefer a career in these particular specialties even though it may not align with population health needs.

The factors influencing specialty choice are multiple and complex. In the case of physicians, the Bland-Meurer model (see figure 3.1) summarizes the major ones: student characteristics, specialty characteristics, and medical school influ-

Figure 3.1   The Bland-Meurer Model of Primary Care Career Choice for Physicians

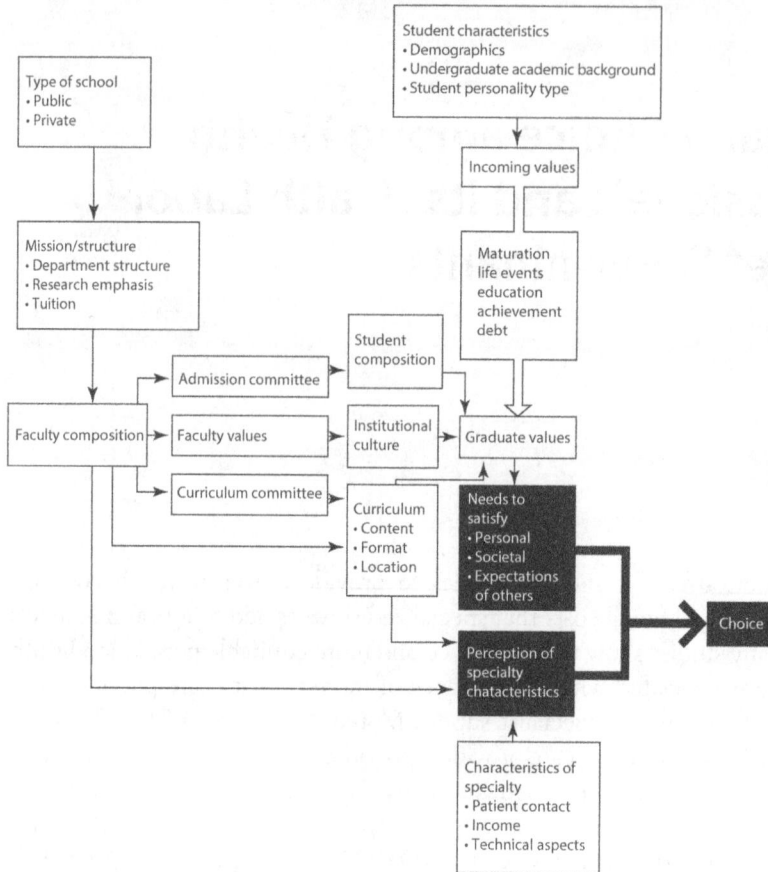

Source: Bland, Meurer, and Maldonado 1995, 623.

ences (Bland, Meurer, and Maldonado 1995). The structure may be applicable to other health professions, but researchers have yet to apply it to them.

The next sections apply the model to examine specialty choice patterns across professions.

Trends in Specialty Preference

Trends in specialty preference vary by health care profession, and most of the literature concerns trends for physicians, dentists, and nurses. The literature for high-income countries (HICs) shows an increasing trend of health workers specializing in surgical and medical subspecialties and a declining trend in the popularity of general practice, leading to an imbalance between the supply of physician generalists and of specialists. For example, between 1998 and 2004, the proportion of U.S. medical graduates choosing primary care residencies decreased from 50 percent to 40 percent, with the greatest decline in family medicine, which had only 41 percent of the positions filled by U.S. graduates (Schwartz et al. 2005).

Jolly and colleagues report that between 2001 and 2010 there was a 6.3 percent decrease in the number of residents entering primary care in the United States and 45 percent increase in residents entering subspecialties such as dermatology and neurology, and subspecialties of internal medicine and pediatrics (Jolly, Erikson, and Garrison 2013). This has led to the U.S. Institute for Medicine calling for major reforms in graduate medical education, including de-emphasizing subsidized specialized training for physicians.[1]

In the United Kingdom, the proportion of medical graduates choosing general practice decreased from 45 percent in 1983 to 26 percent in 1993 and 23 percent in 2002 (Lambert et al. 1996; Lambert, Goldacre, and Turner 2006). In the early 2000s, only 26–31 percent of U.K. doctors chose general practice, a trend that changed after reforms in 2004 (Lambert and Goldacre 2011) (see the section "Student Characteristics"). In Germany, between 1996 and 2008, the number of specialists increased from 45 percent to 52 percent, while more than 2,000 medical offices for general practitioners (GPs) in the country were vacant at the beginning of 2009 (Kiolbassa et al. 2011). In Canada, the proportion of medical graduates in family medicine residency fell from 32 percent in 1994 to 26 percent in 2004 (Harvey, DesCôteaux, and Banner 2005).

National-level data on specialty preferences in low- and middle-income countries (LMICs) are unavailable but surveys carried out in medical schools and hospitals show high preference of physicians to specialize and low popularity of general practice (Burch et al. 2011; Hayes and Shakya 2013; Almeida-Filho 2011). Less than 10 percent of physicians in emerging markets like the Arab Republic of Egypt, India, Jordan, Tunisia, and Turkey choose family medicine (Nair and Webster 2010). Studies from Nepal and Pakistan suggest that the most preferred specialties of physicians are surgery and internal medicine (and their subspecialties), pediatrics, and obstetrics and gynecology; and that the popularity of subspecialties like orthopedic surgery and cardiology is increasing (Aslam et al. 2011; Hayes and Shakya 2013).

Among dentists, willingness to undertake specialty training appears mixed. A survey of the American Dental Association showed only 24 percent of practicing dentists were specialists (Atchison et al. 2002), while in Saudi Arabia the majority of dentists are specialists, most of them in prosthodontics, restorative dentistry, and general dentistry (Al-Dlaigan et al. 2011). Among dental students in the United Kingdom and United States in recent years, 40–50 percent planned to specialize (Gallagher, Clarke, and Wilson 2008; Dhima et al. 2012).

LMICs, too, seem to be witnessing a growing trend for specialization among dentists, even as a significant proportion of their population is yet to have access to basic dental services. In Mexico, for instance, specialist dentists increased from 5 percent to 11 percent between 2000 and 2008 (González-Robledo, González-Robledo, and Nigenda 2012). Surveys in a public dental university in Brazil show that a majority of students intend to specialize, with orthodontics being the most popular area (Dos Santos et al. 2013).

Among nursing students, the most popular specialty choices globally have traditionally been midwifery and pediatrics, intensive care, and critical care;

psychiatric nursing has been a rare preference, contributing to a broader shortage of mental health care providers (Gouthro 2009; Happell and Gaskin 2013). Gender plays a role: male nurses lean to specialties in intensive care, emergency departments, psychiatry, and operating theaters and are more likely to move into specialized managerial roles earlier in their careers than women (González-Torrente et al. 2012; McWilliams, Schmidt, and Bleich 2013).

Student Characteristics

Gender also plays a role among physicians: evidence from HICs and LMICs show that more men prefer surgical specialties and more women prefer obstetrics and gynecology, and family medicine (Bittaye et al. 2012; Gowin et al. 2014). Women are more likely to consider factors such as flexible and predictable work hours, a shorter residency period, and family commitments than men (Weissman et al. 2012; Lambert et al. 2012). Specialty choice also shows a gender difference, which is highly prominent in, for example, surgery, and obstetrics and gynecology. In France, for example, a 2008 national survey in which 1,780 medical students participated showed significant gender differences in specialty preferences. Among the 8 percent prospective physicians preferring to be pediatricians, 9 percent gynecologists, and 20 percent GPs, the proportions of women were 88 percent, 82 percent, and 77 percent, respectively (Lefevre et al. 2010).

Age plays a role as well: in Canada, prospective physicians preferring general practice tend to be older, with 70 percent of medical students preferring residency in family medicine older than 25 (Gill et al. 2012). This may be linked to the need to join the labor market sooner and pay back student loans, and, often, to meet their family's financial needs (Gagne and Leger 2005).

Individuals more intrinsically motivated and those with rural background are more likely to choose a career in general practice; those whose parents are doctors or come from high-income families are more likely to specialize. For example, in Canada, 47 percent of medical students preferring residency in family medicine had a rural background (Gill et al. 2012); and a medical student having a physician parent in the United States was less likely to choose a generalist/primary care career than one without a physician parent (Jeffe, Whelan, and Andriole 2010).

Academic performance may drive specialty choice as well. Poor academic or exam performers are often relegated to the least popular specialization in countries where physicians compete for residency slots through a common exam. Mexico, for example, has 5,000 specialized residency slots open per year and may have as many as 50,000 GP physician applicants taking the residency placement test (Laurell 2007). A higher score on the exam means candidates are more likely to get their preferred specialty training spot. Evidence from the two countries to its north did not, however, find such an association: academic performance of students in Canada who pursued careers in family medicine was not different from those choosing other specialties; and the specialty choices of medical graduates with better academic performance were similar to all students in the United States (Lind and Cendan 2003; Woloschuk, Wright, and McLaughlin 2011).

The mechanism of financing higher education can affect career choices. Some governments offer free or subsidized education to qualifying students in public universities. Others use cost sharing, such as the addition of a special fee-paying track alongside scholarships, for regularly admitted fee-paying students (for example, Kenya, the Russian Federation); increase tuition fees, where they already exist (for example, United States, Canada); provide student loans (for example, United States); or limit the subsidized fee or free public sector while promoting the private sector to provide higher education (for example, Brazil, Indonesia, the Philippines).

In countries where student loans are common, the effect of medical school debt on medical specialty choices appears mixed. In the United States, higher debt relative to peers at the same institution is associated with less likelihood of a primary care career (Rohlfing et al. 2014). In Canada, student debt prompted students to look for shorter residency programs like family medicine to pay off their debt sooner (Vanasse et al. 2011). Debt influenced both specialty intentions and emigration decisions for junior doctors in New Zealand (Moore et al. 2006).

Governments in LMICs like Nepal offer scholarships and subsidized medical education in public universities for qualifying students. For example, MBBS education in Nepal's public medical schools costs $2,400 for 5.5 years, against $31,000 (30 times per capita gross domestic product [GDP]) in private medical schools. Students in Nepal can also compete to enroll in private medical schools under government scholarships in return for working in public hospitals in rural areas for two years after graduation (Huntington et al. 2012). Similarly, the annual cost of residency training in surgery or anesthesia in Uganda is about $3,500, or 10 times mean annual household income (Dubowitz, Detlefs, and McQueen 2010). Government scholarships for residency programs in Malawi are very limited and competitive. Other physicians have to look for private sponsorship to finance their training. If an opportunity for specialization (scholarship) arises, physicians are likely to pursue it even if the physician had never planned that specialty or if it is irrelevant to the local population's health needs (Bailey et al. 2012).

Specialty Characteristics

Differences in income across specialties are a powerful determinant of health professionals' career choices. (The effect of increase in income on the supply of GPs in the United Kingdom is described in box 3.1.) Some specialties offer more opportunities for dual practice and employment in the private sector, which increases income. In Japan, for example, all specialists have the same income in hospitals but the low number of specialists in radiology and anesthesiology is associated with the difficulty of being self-employed in these specialties (Matsumoto et al. 2010). It is common practice for physicians in Japan who

Box 3.1   Effect of General Practitioners' Reimbursement on Supply in the United Kingdom

The income of GPs in the United Kingdom was low until the early 2000s (Kroneman, Van der Zee, and Groot 2009). The proportion of graduating cohorts in U.K. medical schools choosing general practice had fallen by around half, from 45 percent in 1983 to 23 percent in 2000 (Lambert and Goldacre 2011). In 2004, GPs' reimbursement structure underwent a major reform, helping reverse the decline and taking the rate back up to 26–35 percent (Lambert and Goldacre 2011) (figure B3.1.1a), although it stayed below the target of 50 percent.

Previously, GPs had been reimbursed through a weighted capitation formula, supplemented by additional payments based on specific services provided. The reform introduced additional bonus payments linked to service provision, generating a sharp rise in GPs' annual income (adjusted for inflation) from $80,580 in 2000 to $155,360 in 2005 (Kroneman, Van der Zee, and Groot 2009) (figure B3.1.1b). Between 2000 and 2009, GPs' income rose about 20 percent more than the average income for the population. In 2007, the policy was revised to curb this unexpected increase, but GPs' income stayed relatively high (Kroneman et al. 2013).

Figure B3.1.1a   Proportion of Graduating Cohorts in U.K. Medical Schools Choosing General Practice

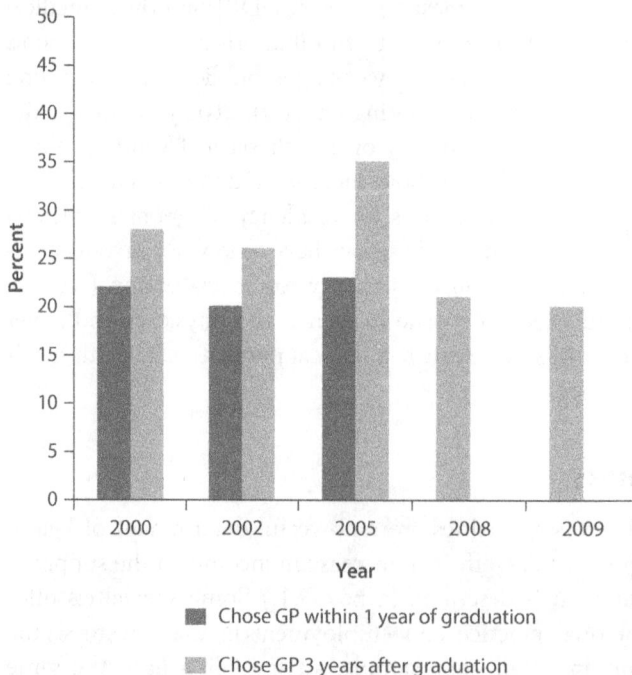

Chose GP within 1 year of graduation

Chose GP 3 years after graduation

Source: Lambert and Goldacre 2011.
Note: GP = general practitioner.

box continues next page

Box 3.1 Effect of General Practitioners' Reimbursement on Supply in the United Kingdom
(continued)

Figure B3.1.1b General Practitioners' Annual Income

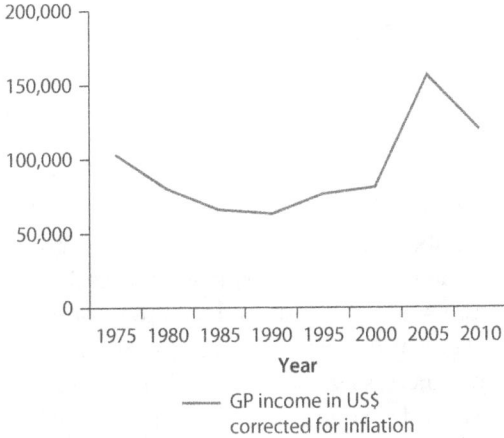

Source: Kroneman, Van der Zee, and Groot 2009; Kroneman et al. 2013.
Note: GP = general practitioner.

The declining trend in general practice popularity in the United Kingdom changed after the health reform that increased general practice income, with 26–35 percent of the graduating cohorts intending to pursue general practice compared to 23 percent before the reform (see figures 3.1 and 4.1) (Lambert and Goldacre 2011). However, the proportion of physicians choosing the specialty is still below the target of 50 percent.

have specialized in hospital-based subspecialties to practice privately (Matsumoto et al. 2010). In countries with a gatekeeping system (such as Denmark and the United Kingdom), the competition for patients between GPs and specialists is less and the income of GPs is higher than in countries without one, like Germany, where patients have direct access to specialists. In 2000, the average annual income of GPs in four European countries (Denmark, Finland, the Netherlands, and the United Kingdom) with a gatekeeping system was about $12,000 more than those in countries without one (Belgium, France, Germany, and Sweden) (Kroneman, Van der Zee, and Groot 2009). General practice income in countries with a strong primary care sector (governance, workforce development, access, and coordination of care) tends to be higher than in those with weak or medium primary care sectors (Kroneman et al. 2013).

In the United States, the median annual incomes of primary care physicians and subspecialists differ hugely: in 2003, that of the former was $150,000 compared with about $400,000 for orthopedic surgeons and radiologists (Wilder et al. 2010). From 1998 to 2000, subspecialists saw their inflation-adjusted income climb by 9 percent and generalists by 2 percent (Schwartz et al. 2005); from 2000 to 2004, the median income for primary care physicians increased by 10 percent, but 16 percent for all other specialists (Bodenheimer, Berenson, and Rudolf 2007). From 1998 to 2004, the proportion of medical graduates pursuing residencies in primary care decreased from 50 percent to 40 percent (Schwartz et al. 2005).

Bodenheimer, Berenson, and Rudolf (2007) attribute three main factors to this widening income in the United States. First, technological advances increase the volume of imaging, diagnostic, and other procedures (performed by specialists) relative to office visits to generalists, thereby increasing the income for specialists. Second, the majority of members in the Relative Value Scale Update Committee (RUC), which is responsible for recommending changes in the reimbursement rate of the major insurers, are specialists, and tend to favor reimbursement rates for specialist services. Third, private insurer payment favors specialty care over primary care, hence increasing income for specialists. (Some of these points have applicability in some developing country settings, as picked up just below.)

Income is not, however, the only factor in physicians' specialty decisions—"prestige" is also important. It is associated with specialties not just with higher earnings but also longer residency period, more competition for residency training spots, and more influence (Creed, Searle, and Rogers 2010). The low prestige ranking and negative portrayal of some specialties can dissuade medical students from pursuing those specialties and create low morale among those who do.

A global[2] systematic review of literature on factors influencing choice of family medicine shows peer pressure and social pressure away from a career in it (Selva et al. 2012). The common perception that general practice is less intellectually challenging and mundane is because GPs treat common illnesses but refer serious ones to specialists. Evidence from Nepal, and Turkey reiterate the perception of general practice as an easy specialty and a back-up option for physicians failing to get into hospital-based specialties (Huda and Yousuf 2006; Hayes and Shakya 2013). Negative portrayal of general practice in medical schools serves to instill these beliefs in medical students (Scott et al. 2007; Selva et al. 2012).

There is increasing evidence from HICs on the influence of quality of life factors, such as lower residency period, predictable work hours, and vacations on physicians' career choice (Pikoulis et al. 2010; Weissman et al. 2012; Abendroth et al. 2014). General practice, for example, gets high lifestyle-friendly rankings in Australia and the United Kingdom (Evans, Lambert, and Goldacre, 2002; Creed et al. 2010). In countries such as Germany, Greece, and the United States, the higher workload of GPs, additional paperwork, and heavier administrative workload make general practice less lifestyle friendly than specialties like ophthalmology, dermatology, or radiology (Mariolis et al. 2007; DeZee et al. 2011;

Gibis et al. 2012). Medical student ranking of lifestyle-friendly specialties in Canada and the United States places radiology, dermatology, anesthesia, and ophthalmology in the higher ranks; obstetrics and gynecology and surgical specialties in low ranks; and primary care specialties as intermediate (Marschall and Karimuddin 2003; Newton, Grayson, and Thompson 2005). Evidence from the United Kingdom reinforces this: doctors reported that their choice for general practice was more for lifestyle than professional reasons (Evans, Lambert, and Goldacre 2002).

School Characteristics

The availability of training programs is an obvious determinant of career choice. In Japan, training in primary care and residency programs in general practice is unavailable (Koike et al. 2010). In LMICs, the number of postgraduate programs and specialty options is limited, which influences students' choices. For example, medical students in Nepal reported that acceptance in an available program was the most important determinant of career choice (Hayes and Shakya 2013). In Sub-Saharan Africa, there are 168 medical schools producing about 10,000–11,000 graduates a year; 58 schools are reported to have postgraduate programs, and these can only accept 25 percent of medical graduates (Mullan et al. 2011). In Nepal the number of residency slots available is about 20 percent of the number of graduates (Hayes and Shakya 2013).

Some schools appear to produce a higher proportion of graduates choosing careers in general practice than other schools. In the United States, for example, graduates from publicly funded medical schools are more likely to pursue family medicine or primary care residency than those from private medical schools (Jeffe, Whelan, and Andriole 2010; Mullan et al. 2010). The private sector in Brazil promotes an individualistic ideology with a hospital-oriented and specialization-driven pattern of medical education that does not prepare the ideal graduate to work in the country's public health system (Almeida-Filho 2011). In India, one study found no difference in career intentions among public and private medical school students (Diwan et al. 2013). In Pakistan, the top three specialty choices of students and graduates in public and private medical schools were similar, but those in private schools expressed more interest in subspecialties like cardiology and orthopedics (Aslam et al. 2011).

Experience during training seems to have a great influence on career choice. Schools producing more family health practitioners have more mandatory clinical rotations in family medicine and primary care and better perception of clinical competence of the family medicine faculty (Scott et al. 2007; Erikson et al. 2013), which may be summarized as a "hidden curriculum," defined as a "set of influences that function within the organizational structure and culture" (Woloschuk, Wright, and McLaughlin 2011). Mullan and colleagues' study of the social mission of medical school shows that elite medical schools in the United States do a poor job of producing primary care physicians perhaps due to the emphasis on technical education, research, and specialization (Mullan et al. 2010).

Notes

1. http://www.nap.edu/download.php?record_id=18754.
2. Ten studies from six countries (Australia, Canada, Japan, Spain, United Kingdom, and United States) were included.

CHAPTER 4

The Value of Health Professional Education

Alternative Cadres

In many countries, mid-level providers play a major role in providing basic health services, and in some countries provide even specialist services (Lassi et al. 2013; Rao et al. 2013). Health workforce policy makers increasingly view mid-level providers—with their shorter period of training—as a cost-effective way to deliver basic health care services. Analytically this can be taken as a labor market adjustment either due to shortages of higher-level cadres (there is a need to fulfill the demand for health workers and ultimately health care) or due to limited ability to pay (demand) for higher cadres (usually rural, remote, and poorer areas where funding for health workers is limited).

Several studies have sought to evaluate the contribution of alternative cadres, and a growing body of evidence has demonstrated the value of these cadres and their ability to improve patient outcomes in primary care and other settings (Halter et al. 2013; Lassi et al. 2013; Rao et al. 2013; van Ginneken et al. 2011). The shorter training time for these providers has helped improve health systems capacity to respond to demands for preventive and primary care services. The human immunodeficiency virus/acquired immune deficiency syndrome (HIV/AIDS) epidemic in Sub-Saharan Africa provides the best example of how mid-level provider roles emerged and enabled primary care and obstetric services to expand (Blaauw et al. 2013; George, Gow, and Bachoo 2013).

Estimated Rates of Return to Health Professional Education

Rates of return to education (RORE) can be considered as the stream of goods and services that flow over time in response to an educational investment. The individual graduate of an educational program, or the graduate's family or other personal sponsor, has invested time, effort, and, in most cases, finance to reach the point of graduation, representing the private cost.

The *private return* to that investment is an expected stream of increased income relative to that expected in the absence of that education, and other personal benefits such as more interesting or agreeable work, higher status, or higher quality of life. The private rate of return expresses the value of the annual additional flow of personal benefits as a proportion of the initial outlay in private cost.

There are also publicly borne costs and publicly accrued benefits associated with education. In most countries much of the educational process from childhood to higher degree level is publicly subsidized, so that much of the financial cost of education is paid through public resources. The *public return* to education consists of the public benefits associated with a more educated population. These include the value to the whole of society of the services delivered by educated people, including skilled health care professionals. They also include more intangible benefits, such as benefits to arts and culture. The private and public returns to education combined constitute the *social return* to education.

The public and social returns to investment in health professional education present particular complexities in the key calculation of the value of skilled health care professionals' services. The value of an effective health system is vast in terms of its ability to meet needs and demands for preventive, promotive, curative, and rehabilitative services. Nevertheless, the difficulties of estimating that value as a whole and of attributing elements of that overall value to the investment in the formation of specific cadres of health professional are considerable. The current evidence base allows at best estimates of the partial value of some health professional education investments, such as the value of increasing nursing specialization for health outcomes of patients in specific hospital wards.

RORE are estimated by comparing the earning streams of those who do and do not achieve successive levels of education and expressing the difference as a rate of return on the outlay invested in educational costs. This assumes that the higher earnings of more educated people reflect the contribution made by the investment in education (private and social costs). The measured rate of return is used to measure both the private return to the individual, which is expected to predict the educational investment, and the career choice of the individual. It is also often assumed to proxy for the social return on the basis that higher earnings reflect higher productivity.

Yet, RORE are not without problems. Early on, Blaug summed up what are still the major objections to the RORE approach, the most important of which is perhaps the difficulty of "unpacking" the contribution of education and other factors in determining future earnings (Blaug 1968). As well as enhancing a set of skills, the processes of student selection of courses and admission officials' selection of students to courses usually ensure that those already showing signs of aptitude, or having acquired related skills, are selected. It is then difficult to distinguish between the value of the skills selected for and the value of the enhanced skill. Other variables that may also be intercorrelated with education and earnings include motivation and social class.

Other objections largely concern the interpretation of the RORE estimate. As seen, while financial returns are important in career and education choices, other variables—ranging from altruism to lifestyle preferences—also matter. And while education matters for its contribution to career opportunities, it also has consumption value in its own right. Hence, interpreting RORE as the full private return to education is inaccurate.

It is also inaccurate to interpret RORE as the social return to education, in that higher earnings might not reflect higher productivity. Labor markets are imperfect in capturing productivity levels in the wage rate for several reasons (the most important for health labor markets are discussed in the following section). Further, the principal benefits of an educated population are to society as a whole and not captured at the individual level. A final objection is that the current career opportunities of those educated in the past are poor guides to the future career opportunities of those educated now, owing to significant changes in education and the labor market in the periods involved.

Despite these difficulties, RORE remain a common approach to evaluating educational investments and the prediction of student choices among educational opportunities and of careers. Methodological developments tackle the typology of issues set out by Blaug (1968), particularly the endogeneity problem (Blaug 1968; Dickson and Harmon 2011).

The literature on health professional education (appendix B) variously investigates the private and social costs of health professional education; the private and social returns to health professional education; and either the rates of return or cost-benefit ratios. ("Cost-benefit" or "cost-effectiveness" terminology is the more common term applied when social rates of return are the question of interest—the principle is the same.) In principle, social costs, returns, and rates of return sum to private and public costs and benefits. In practice, the public perspective (public cost) is often reported separately and a full social analysis is rarely undertaken (as reflected in the appendix).

Methodological issues identified in costing medical education usually arise from allocating the costs of teaching hospitals between patient care and student education. Bicknell (2001), for example, used the approach of "detailed discussion" with staff in a Vietnamese teaching hospital to determine the primary purpose of activity to derive an allocation formula. Most studies consider the cost of training a health professional to be those associated with years of health professional training, but Mills et al. (2011) consider the costs to be all educational investment, including basic schooling of the graduating health professional. Literature focused on Africa has estimated approximate costs of medical education by dividing total annual public expenditure on medical schools by the number of annual graduates (Hagopian et al. 2005; Mills et al. 2011) or by proposing that fees set for students intended not to be subsidized can proxy for social cost (Kirigia et al. 2006).

As shown in appendix B, few studies consider private and social (or public) costs to compare their relative levels. Bicknell (2001) excluded all private costs in his analysis of the returns to Vietnamese medical education. Namate (1995) included both in her analysis of Malawian midwifery education and found that private costs amounted to about 16 percent of the total and were dominated by opportunity (or value of time) costs, which accounted for 91 percent of student costs (Namate 1995). Clearly, the distribution of costs between institutions and students, and of private costs between time and financial costs, are both contingent on the cost-sharing model or the level of tuition fees. Namate (1995) does not discuss this, and it appears that at the time the Malawian nursing and midwifery training courses for which she estimated costs did not charge tuition fees, suggesting that these shares are likely to be at the lower end of private costs in total, and of financial costs in total private expenditures.

In the United States, all those who have reported on tuition fees for medical education agree that they have been increasing in real terms over the period of the published literature. Increases in the range of 51–93 percent between 1995 and 2004 versus 24 percent in the consumer price index over the same period are reported (Kerr and Brown 2006). This literature raises concerns about the resulting levels of indebtedness of medical graduates and about some of the implications of specialty choice (see chapter 2). Increasing fees appear to reflect rising costs, which, some argue, relate to length and intensity of training and the pressures on both arising from a growing body of medical knowledge (Jones and Korn 1997). It has been suggested that returns can be improved and costs reduced by shortening tuition-based training for undergraduates (Doroghazi and Alpert 2014).

In Canada and the United States, the increased demand for entry-level nursing personnel generated the accelerated bachelor's degree program in nursing and increased the RORE for this profession. Designed for individuals who possess a bachelor's degree in another field, students can complete a bachelor's degree in nursing in 12–24 months of full-time, year-round study. These programs have increased nursing bachelor's degree enrollees in both countries. In the United States, production levels of nursing personnel have reached sustainable levels for the first time in three decades (Auerbach, Buerhaus, and Staiger 2011).

Papers that focused on compensation of health professionals raised concerns about the implications for recruitment arising from differences between comparable professions and between specialties. These mostly concern medicine and conclude that it is poorly remunerated relative to other professions (Kahn et al. 2006) and that primary care is poorly remunerated relative to other specialties (Weeks et al. 1994; Weeks and Wallace 2002a, 2002b, 2002c). Spetz and Bates (2013) conclude that obtaining a baccalaureate after a degree in nursing increases gross lifetime earnings by up to 5.1 percent (Spetz and Bates 2013). Economic crises, however, can shift labor market outcomes even for bachelor-prepared nurses through delayed hiring (Buerhase, Auerbach, and Staiger 2007; Buchan, O'May, and Dussault 2013). In some studies (Simon, Dranove, and White 1998; Luiz and Bahia 2009), the focus included consideration of the impact of policy or health systems change on earnings of health professionals or on differences between the private and public sectors (Nash and Pfeifer 2006) or urban and rural careers (Reschovsky and Staiti 2005). The complexity of income sources in some contexts, especially those of multiple job holding, limits the confidence in some income estimates (for example, Luiz and Bahia 2009). A number of reports suggest a decline over the long term in doctors' relative incomes (Burstein and Cromwell 1985; McManus 2005), though shorter-term comparisons for a wider range of health professionals are unsurprisingly inconclusive (Luiz and Bahia 2009).

Few cost analyses have considered scale effects. Emery et al. (2006) suggest that the expansion of a small postgraduate program recruiting international medical graduates in Canada exhibited gains of scale, that is, when the number of residency positions increased from 8 to 12 over 2003/04, the estimated annual cost fell from C$85,064 to C$60,942 per graduate (Emery et al. 2006). Newbold (2008) considers scale effects in the returns to education as a whole (in contrast to scale effects in the training production function), citing studies that have estimated diminishing returns to numbers of nurses in the workforce and to the proportion of those who are graduates (Newbold 2008). Such effects are likely to be context specific; for example, one underlying explanation was that as the numbers of nurses increased, nurses started to undertake tasks that those with lower qualifications could have undertaken. This seems likely to be conditional on the overall balance of skill levels in the workforce, although it logically applies everywhere on the economist's assumption of "all else equal"—holding everything else including numbers of staff of other skill levels and patient characteristics constant.

In calculating private rates of return, most studies report raw salary differences between the health professional group of interest and others, expressed as an annual percentage return on investment in the additional education required. Others adjust for hours worked (for example, Weeks et al. 1994; Weeks and Wallace 2002b). Despite the largely negative conclusions of the literature on incomes in terms of both trends and relative levels, most studies conclude that rates of return for the United States are positive (appendix C). Yet, there are clear gaps in coverage and difficulties in making comparisons between the estimates shown in the annex. Most rates of return fall between 14 percent and 22 percent for all time periods, excluding Weeks and Wallace's (2002a, 2002c) retrospective estimates for 1992, which are all above 22 percent except for primary care. The same authors' estimates for orthopedics and urology in 1998 remain above 22 percent. Their estimate for primary care in 1998 is far below all other estimates, at 3 percent.

Hagemeier and Murawski (2011) support the above evidence of falling incomes and rising costs by reporting a downward trend in the rate of return (Hagemeier and Murawski 2011). This was earlier discerned by Weeks and Wallace (2002a, 2002b, 2002c) in comparison with Weeks et al. (1994). Weeks and Wallace (2002c) analysis is probably the most consistent and comprehensive analysis of trends in the United States (summarized in figure 4.1). In contrast, however, Weeks and Wallace (2003) conclude that medical incomes have not been declining for general/family practice, general surgery, obstetrics and

Figure 4.1   The Hours-adjusted Internal Rate of Return on Additional Training for Five Surgical Specialties and Primary Care Medicine

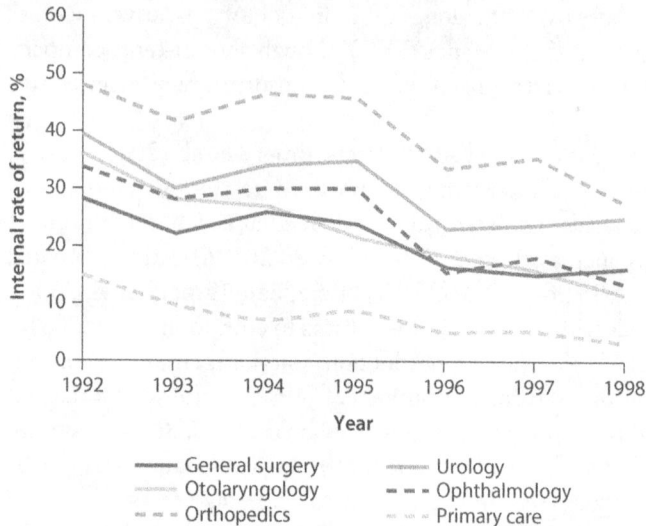

Source: Reprinted from Weeks and Wallace 2002c, 797.

gynecology, general internal medicine, or pediatrics, implying that their rate of return analysis is primarily driven by increasing costs of medical and specialty education (Weeks and Wallace 2003).

The literature evaluating the social costs and benefits of training programs is even more limited than that evaluating private costs and benefits. However, for example, a family medicine training program in Oklahoma, United States, was calculated to have generated a $370 million return from a $139 million investment (Lapolla et al. 2004). A medical school in the Philippines, founded on very low financial costs (though these are not described in detail and social costs are not recognized), had apparently impressive results in a "very cost-effective model of producing rural doctors" (Cristobal and Worley 2012). In Australia, Flinders University's approach to using alternative settings for clinical education was found to be academically effective and economically affordable (Couper and Worley 2010).

The medical school of the University of the Transkei in South Africa has achieved good academic standards while ensuring that a high level of medical graduates choose practice in rural areas (Kwizera, Igumbor, and Mazwai 2005). The authors of an evaluation of the cost-effectiveness of in-service nurse-midwifery training in Indonesia were able to estimate the cost of each percentage point score increase in a competency test, but not to further project the implications for health outcomes (Walker et al. 2002). Another paper on the cost-effectiveness of education, this time for rural service, concluded that the costs of rural dental service provision in Australia were slightly higher when provided by students than salaried staff. Even though the value of services was also higher, the impact on encouraging rural practice was excluded from the analysis (Richards et al. 2002).

In nursing and pharmacy, researchers have compared a wide range of educational programs, producing a wider range of results than in medicine, including some negative values with a lower median. Perhaps all that can be concluded is that rates of return are sensitive to estimation approach, may be profession specific, and are far from stable over time. For example, Emery and colleagues conduct an analysis from the perspective of the Canadian public sector, rather than a full social cost analysis, of a program recruiting international medical graduates and found that the public investment of hiring foreign graduates generates a return of 9–13 percent in savings relative to training and recruiting Canadian doctors (Emery et al. 2006). Yet, this ignores costs and benefits beyond Canada's borders.

Overall, the attempts to measure social costs and benefits or rates of return to social investment have major limitations that no doubt reflect the complexity of the task. In particular, computing the social returns to more or better health professional education would require an understanding of the relationship between "more" and "better" health professional education and health outcomes.

CHAPTER 5

The Market for Health Professional Education

Linked Markets: Health Professional Education and Health Care

To illustrate market links between educational and health care systems, the U.S. model serves as the example for this section (as the only country for which there is enough literature). The system and incentives for the supply of medical education in the United States is explained by Schroeder (1993) and McEldowney and Berry (1995) and has changed little in the last 20 years. Academic health centers dominate control over the medical education system, producing all U.S.–trained physicians and controlling the bulk of residency positions through their teaching hospitals. Although other bodies are involved in the governance of the system, these bodies are dominated by academic faculty, giving academic health centers essentially monopolistic control over the system (Schroeder 1993). The costs of residencies are covered through charges for patient care at university hospitals, which are augmented by reimbursement surcharges for the costs of medical training and additional public insurance payments that directly cover a proportion of residents' stipends. These incentives resulted in available residency positions equal to 135 percent of U.S. medical school graduates in the 1990s, the gap filled by international medical graduates. While a more recent estimate of the subsidy level was not found, the proportion of residency positions filled by international medical graduates remained fairly constant at about 27 percent between 2001/02 and 2012/13, suggesting that the incentives did not change much (Brotherton and Etzel 2007).

The effects of this system in producing a surplus of (over-) qualified physicians and an imbalance between generalists and specialists are well documented. Schroeder (1993) reported that while specialists generally constituted 25–50 percent of the medical workforce in European countries, in the United States the proportion was over 70 percent. In the mid-1990s, there was some optimism that the growing influence and importance of managed care would provide the market discipline that would resolve the problem. Foreman made the optimists' case: "the perverse incentives that made physicians unbridled cost generators will vanish" (Foreman 1996, 244). One paper found that growth of generalists was positively correlated and growth of specialists negatively correlated with managed care penetration between 1985 and 1994, providing some supportive evidence (Jiang and Begun 2002). It is therefore unclear whether it was the retreat from managed care of the late 1990s or the failure of managed care to resolve the critical market failures involved that explains the persistent imbalance 20 years later. The continued imbalance between generalists and specialists remains well documented by, for example (Julian, Riegels and Baron 2011; Hing and Schappert 2012; Shipman et al. 2013) despite the expected pressures of recent U.S. reforms on primary care systems (Long 2008; Long and Massi 2009).[1]

The extent to which market forces discipline the tendency of medical education systems in other parts of the world to overproduce specialists varies. Mexico, for example, has significant unemployment among general practitioners (GPs) (Nigenda, Ruiz, and Bjarano 2005), while Nicaragua, with a system that produces an outlying proportion of specialists by Latin American standards, has almost full employment (Nigenda and Machado 2000).

While the institutional arrangements governing medical education in the United States are atypical of the rest of the world, which is characterized in general by much more government intervention and planning of training places for all types of health professional, its case illustrates that health care markets may not be reliable in sending signals via rates of return to different types of health professional education that encourage growth in shortage occupations and discourage entry to surplus ones.

The market for health professional education and its links to the market for health care has a web of interrelationships (figure 5.1). Analysis can shed light on the market situations of different types of health professional education systems in different countries, although the literature coverage is patchy. The expected relationships could be expressed in terms of demand and supply curves, at least in relation to evaluated need, the difference between need and demand representing the information problem (to some degree at least).

The key relationship, which may be failing to regulate the medical education market according to the earlier discussion, is the one between shortage/surplus and compensation. Other market mechanisms have been shown to behave normally: for example, subsidizing nursing education increases the supply of nurses (Eastaugh 1985), and Leffler and Lindsay (1981) found expected relationships between the market for medical care and the market for medical education, supporting the applicability of traditional economics to the health sector (Leffler and Lindsay 1981). While these findings relate to an earlier stage of evolution of the U.S. health system, physician control over patient demand was relatively unchallenged at that time.

The literature best enables the interrelationships in the figure to be illustrated with examples from nursing, although it seems a matter of logic that the variables are equally relevant for all health (and perhaps other) professions. At the center of the market for nursing education is its supply, represented in the figure by educational institutional capacity and its demand—"applicant numbers" in

Figure 5.1   Interrelationships between Health Professional Job Market and Health Professional Education Market

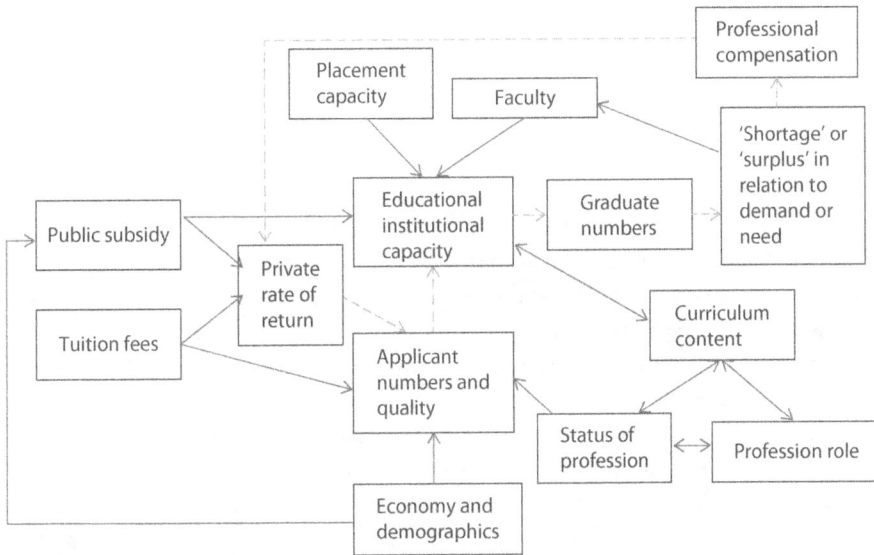

Source: World Bank.
Note: The dotted arrows indicate the core demand and supply elements and links between the health professional education and health care markets.

the figure. The balance between these is variable for nursing. In Nigerian nursing schools, for example, demand for places by qualified candidates outstrips supply (Ayandiran et al. 2013).

An examination of U.S. nursing school supply demonstrates shifting demand over 30 years: Eastaugh (1985) described a situation in the 1980s of "excess schools" in the United States, and this led to multiple school closures in the early 1990s. With the resurgence of a domestic U.S. nursing shortage in the early 2000s, this situation no longer prevailed by 2005 (Department of Health and Human Services 2005). In Australia, by contrast, one paper attributes expansion constraints to the lack of nursing training "placements" (supervised practice positions for students) (Preston 2009).

As with doctors, the key market outcome of "shortage" or "surplus" relates not only to overall numbers of nurses, but numbers playing particular roles. Sochalski and Weiner (2011) report in the United States that a small and declining proportion of registered nurses are working in primary care settings even as the number of primary care nurse practitioner jobs continues to increase. The relationship between perceived shortages evaluated from a public health perspective for primary care roles along with the removal of regulatory constraints that limit the scope of practice and compensation levels—an imbalance that a well-functioning market would rectify—appears of similar character to that for doctors discussed above. Patient demands and insurance reimbursements (their relative roles varying with context) fail to flow according to the needs of public health (see figure 1.1), ensuring that the workforce imbalance persists largely due to market protectionist actions by dominant professional groups. More recent reforms to the U.S. system would appear to require the expansion of the primary care system, but it is not clear that the health care market is responding yet to achieve that end (Sochalski and Weiner 2011).

A contrasting case emerges in former Soviet Union states, where the reorientation of health care systems implied a retreat from extreme and legally enforced specialization for doctors and the transformation of nurses from a low-status and low-skilled profession in Soviet hospitals (Parfitt 2009). A similar evolution took place in Nigeria, from "*gallipot* nurses" (trained to recognize equipment) to "yes doctor" nurses (trained to assist doctors), to technical nurses (trained to operate independently) (Ayandiran et al. 2013). Such progress in their professional role is seen across the world and adds complexity to the forces shaping demand and supply of nursing education. These are represented by a triad of factors: "curriculum content," "status of profession," and "profession role" at the bottom right of figure 5.1. The transition cannot occur without a modernization of curricula, yet modernization is challenging, while the main candidates for faculty positions are those who have graduated from the old system and when employers may not accept the rationale. These factors may bear some responsibility for Nigeria's difficulties with this process (Ayandiran et al. 2013). Trends in the status of nursing do not appear to be monotonic, however (box 5.1).

In settings in which nurse employment is predominantly public, relative salaries and public subsidies to nursing education decline when public finances are

---

Box 5.1   How Demographics and Positioning of the Nursing Profession Can Interrelate, Israel

In Israel, a measure of occupational prestige associated with registered and practical nurses declined between 1972 and 1992 by about 8 percentage points for both. Two papers focus on the trends in applicants for a nursing school in Haifa in relation to economic and demographic change in that city, which has a predominantly Jewish population but a large minority of Palestinians who are discriminated against in the Israeli labor market. The city has also seen waves of immigration from the former Soviet Union.

The authors suggests that strong demand for nursing training is contingent on the existence of a population for whom the profession offers a springboard for upward mobility, something judged to be a transitional stage. As a population becomes better established, it begins to invest more in longer, higher prestige and more remunerative training opportunities. Bachelor-level education can be an important factor associated with professional prestige because of the degree's association with economic mobility. Birenbaum-Carmeli (2002) suggests that these types of relationship between educational opportunities, immigrant adaptation, and labor market politics may be common, if less pronounced, in other settings.

Source: Birenbaum-Carmeli 2002; Birenbaum-Carivieli 2007.

under pressure. Tuition fees may increase in tandem, combining to reduce private rates of return. Yet, since these conditions usually coincide with economic downturn, rates of return may also be depressed in alternative professions, protecting nursing markets from significant adverse effects. A similar account is given of the United States in the Reagan era (Eastaugh 1985), though a more recent analysis of the 2008 economic crisis on the nursing profession in OECD countries suggests that the long-term implications for nursing workforce shortages are likely in most countries (Buchan, O'May, and Dussault 2013). The major influences are declining real nursing pay in the wake of "austerity" measures affecting the health sector, international migration to countries in which such measures have been least extended, and movement out of the health sector toward those less affected by such measures. The trends in availability and uptake of nursing training opportunities were not analyzed, however.

Public financial stringency in England reveals issues with attempts to reshape professional roles and curricula for specialist community public health nurses (SCPHNs) (Lindley, Sayer, and Thurtle 2011). Employment of SCPHNs—formerly known as health visitors but now with a broader scope of practice—declined by 14 percent between 1999 and 2008, and student numbers declined by 30 percent in the latter five years of that period. The authors suggest that such public health roles typically fare badly in such periods, evaluation here is hampered by the SCPHNs' increased workload and responsibility. Competition for places on SCPHN courses is "varied," presumably reflecting the balance between rates of return in this and other occupations, nationally.

Some of these issues are explored in relation to dentistry in the United States by Nash and Brown (2012). Dentistry education in the United States is subsidized and regulated, but the subsidy is declining and tuition fees are increasing, as was reported for medicine in the United States in chapter 4. Nevertheless, an excess demand for places is described, implying that graduate numbers are not so sensitive to these changes to the rate of return to dental education that dentistry has become unattractive.

Privatization of Health Professional Education in LMICs

The research shaping the previous discussion largely ignores the question of ownership of health care training and education institutions, but identifies some issues of incentives and financing. As with other areas of the public–private mix in health care, one must distinguish the roles of public and private ownership from those of public and private financing and of more and less market orientation of institutions, whether formally public or private. For example, a not-for-profit institution may be private, but genuinely motivated by public service, and a publicly owned institution may be exposed to strong market forces so that its behavior is indistinguishable from a for-profit institution. Both publicly and privately owned institutions can in principle be subsidized by the state and/or funded through tuition fees. Private schools in high-income countries (HICs) are usually state funded and nonprofit; in low- and middle-income countries (LMICs), they tend to be dependent on tuition fees and be profit oriented (Siribaddana, Agampoidi, and Siribaddana 2012). This section is concerned with the issues of the latter type of medical college in LMICs.

Few data exist on trends in LMIC private sector training schools. For medical education at least, the phenomenon is relatively new in Africa, emerging in the 1990s and strengthening since 2000 (figure 5.2) (Mullan et al. 2011).

In Asia, the private sector has made highly variable incursions into medical training (Shehnaz 2011): India has the most private medical schools in the world; more than half of schools in Bangladesh, Japan, the Democratic People's Republic of Korea, Nepal, Pakistan, and Taiwan, China are private; the Islamic Republic of Iran and Mongolia have far fewer private medical training institutions; and China, Israel, the Democratic People's Republic of Korea, Kuwait, Myanmar, Sri Lanka, Thailand, and Vietnam have none. In the Middle East, most countries have either wholly or mainly privatized their medical training sector.

Kenya, South Africa, and Thailand (and India) are seeing a rising private role in nurse production (Reynolds et al. 2013). In South Africa, for example, the proportion of nurses graduating from private institutions increased from 45 percent in 2001 to 66 percent in 2004, and in Thailand, from 20 percent in 2001 to 24 percent in 2010. In Kenya, 35 out of 68 nursing institutions were privately run in 2009/10.

India is the country best documented on the growth of private medical education and exemplifies some concerns, such as rapid private expansion, inadequate and corrupted regulation, and poor quality of education. Mahal and Mohanan (2006) offer the most comprehensive analysis of such growth there, showing trends in enrollment capacity and number of institutions between 1950 and

Figure 5.2 Founding Dates of Medical Schools in Sub-Saharan Africa by Sector

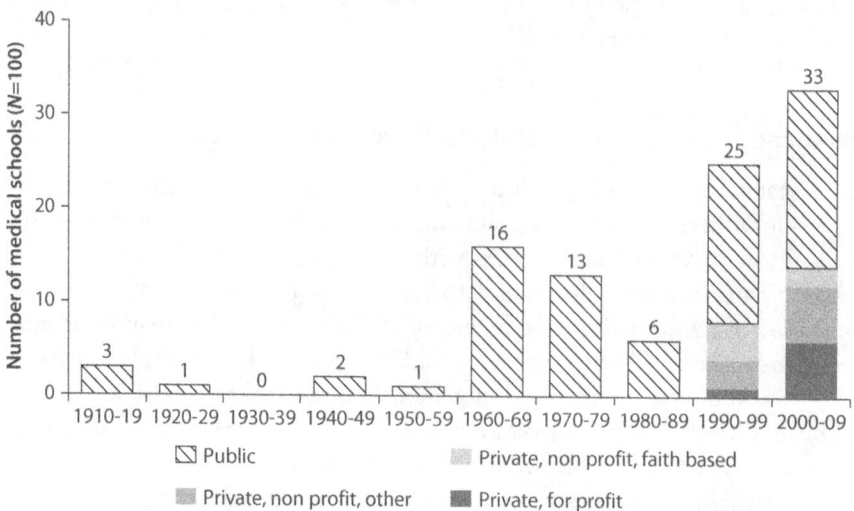

Source: Mullan et al. 2011, 1115.

2004. The former increased more than fivefold and the latter nearly eightfold to 221 from 28 over the period, taking the proportion of private enrollment, and institution numbers increased from a negligible 1.4 percent to around 45 percent (Mahal and Shah 2006). (Over the same period, India's population increased around threefold.)[2] A more recent paper reports an increase in the number of teaching institutions from 284 colleges in 2009 to 335 colleges in 2011 and indicates that this growth in institution numbers was in the private sector (which constituted more than 50 percent of the total by 2011) (Ananthakrishnan and Shanthi 2012).

A couple of commentators attribute the growth of private institutions to the economic transition, starting in the 1980s (Nagral 2010; Das 2012). Yet, Mahal and Mohanan (2006)'s numbers suggest that by 1980 the private sector contribution had grown to 13.7 percent of enrollments and 12.7 percent of institutions indicating earlier roots.

Ananthakrishnan (2007) estimates the implications of the growth in numbers on the need for faculty and suggests that the faculty shortfall in "most departments" is 20–25 percent, a problem identified elsewhere (Ananthakrishnan 2007; Yatish and Manjula 2010). Faculty shortages obviously raise concerns about quality (discussed below). They also clarify a link between private and public institutions, as the demand for faculty among the former can attract staff from the latter. Some specialties in which the shortage is most acute include forensic medicine and radio diagnosis, such that faculty salaries are driven up in these areas and the public sector's regulated pay scales cannot compete (Joseph, Babu, and Sharmila 2010). Not only do faculty shortfalls in the public sector result (especially in sectors with acute shortages) but the public, regulated systems (which set pay scales by seniority rather than market forces) are undermined.

Despite quite an extensive regulatory framework, the literature suggests that regulation fails to assure quality in private medical education (and may also fail to do so in the public sector) due to capacity and governance shortfalls. The task of regulation is complex in a large country with a mix of regulatory responsibilities between federal and state levels. The national regulatory body, the Medical Council of India, for example, issues licenses for private medical colleges on the basis of "no-objection certificates" provided by states, pursuant to analysis of need at local level. Both levels are criticized for the Council's "archaic regulations" (Ananthakrishnan 2010), outright corruption (Kumar 2004; Yathish and Manjula 2010; Nagral 2010), and poor enforcement and variable standards applying to the issuing of no-objection certificates (Ananthakrishnan and Shanthi 2012), resulting in 172 out of 299 medical colleges in 2009 being concentrated in just six states, in which only 29 percent of the Indian population reside.

Other LMICs have much less literature on medical education but some evidence suggests that problems of competition between private medical schools by grade inflation, for example, occur elsewhere, as in Nepal (Shankar and Thapa 2010). Concerns about the pace of change and the maintenance of standards have also been expressed in Malaysia (Abdul Hamid 2000).

For private nursing training, Adhikari (2010) provides a single but detailed source on the situation in Nepal (Adhikari 2010). After licensing regulations were introduced in 1989, providers grew rapidly from before 1989 to the time of writing: from 5 to 40 institutions for auxiliary nurse-midwives, from 6 to 39 institutions for proficiency certificate-level nurses ("staff nurses"), from 1 to 17 institutions for B.Sc Nursing graduates, 14 programs for Bachelor of Nursing graduates, and 3 programs for M.Sc Nursing graduates (numbers of Bachelor of Nursing and M.Sc Nursing programs prior to 1989 are not provided). Some of India's medical education issues find echoes in her analysis, such as quality shortfalls among faculty.

In common with the earlier account of constraints to nurse education in Australia (Preston 2009), Adhikari (2010) describes opportunities for placements as a key obstacle to developing the private sector and a subsidiary market in placement opportunities, capable of producing wards with more students than hospital beds. Adhikari also finds some evidence of corruption in the governance system, licensing authority, external examination system, and among college principles. She offers an explanation of how the system allows these outcomes (box 5.2).

Box 5.2 Market Failure in Nepal

The problem is not apparently primarily one of information (Adhikari 2010). Course applicants understand that many private institutions are second class, and, at the time of the research, graduates of these institutions were protesting their treatment as second-class health workers.

However, demand for places in nursing training vastly outstripped supply in public institutions, perceived in contrast as first class in the national context (40–45 places were reported as receiving 548–3,000 applications), and high fees at private institutions (£2,500–3,500 a year, or roughly eight times Nepal's 2011 per capita gross domestic product (GDP).[a] Such high demand was linked to expectations of working abroad, and indeed curricula of both public and private training institutions were reformed explicitly to cater to the international market (and to include geriatric and mental health nursing specialties, neither of which is much practiced in Nepal).

The market failure appears rooted in the absence of an adequate supply of reputable training opportunities despite the recognition of quality levels by the consumers of nursing education, which would be expected to yield a price premium to a private sector supplier able to provide a higher quality program. This might be explained by market failures to supply capital to potentially reputable private sector providers or by the difficulties of signaling higher quality to potential foreign employers which would produce a "market for lemons" (Akerlof 1970), an information problem associated not with the immediate customers of nursing schools but with the next (health care) market in the derivation chain.

Source: http://data.un.org/CountryProfile.aspx?crName=Nepal consulted May 9, 2014, around £360; www.xe.com consulted May 9, 2014.

a. Reported 2011 Nepal per capita GDP of $607.

In their literature review of India, Kenya, the Philippines, South Africa, and Thailand, Reynolds et al. (2013) find common concerns over quality, with 61 percent of nursing colleges in India reported unsuitable for training nurses by one study (Reynolds et al. 2013). In Thailand, a study judged that graduate quality was lower among privately trained students (perhaps because lower-quality students are accepted). In Kenya, a study reported that the tutor-to-student ratio was nearly three times higher in private than public training institutions. The authors also report evidence from the Philippines that fewer than 50 percent of private school graduates passed licensing exams between 2005 and 2007.

Notes

1. http://www.nap.edu/download.php?record_id=18754.
2. http://www.un.org/esa/population/publications/WPP2004/2004Highlights_finalrevised.pdf (accessed April 21, 2014).

CHAPTER 6

Discussion

The context of the formation of health professionals from school graduates to university postgraduates and onto their entry into the health workforce is subject to rapid change, with roots in multiple epidemiological, social, economic, political, and technological processes. The wide range of contexts in which the literature reviewed has been produced and of the health professions in question has given rise to diverse phenomena, some supporting and some undermining populations' access to appropriate and effective services. In all of these phenomena, the role played by markets is clear, and the process through which failures in the health care market are replicated in the health labor market and in turn in the operations of health education and training markets are identifiable.

Stakeholders in health professional education have a complex task of managing market forces that generally fail to support the production and allocation of health professionals to meet public health–evaluated need. Examples from the above text are legion, but dominant is the failure of wage rates to respond to shortage and thereby to send appropriate signals through private rates of return to those making choices among training programs and careers. A common phenomenon over time and across contexts is the market's tendency to overvalue specialist skills, resulting in demand for specialist education that in turn generates imbalances in the workforce and hence overmedicalized, hospital-centric health care systems. This phenomenon is reinforced by processes that allocate status and prestige to specialist occupations—and their opposites to generalists. Crucially, these processes are in training schools, where a "hidden curriculum" may often send these messages. These processes appear equally identifiable in the health systems of high-, medium-, and low-income countries.

The attempt to balance overspecialized medical professionals by the introduction of mid-level cadres appears a somewhat successful strategy in a number of contexts. In the United States, the mid-level cadre is the nurse-practitioner or physician assistant, now employed and accepted in multiple roles from primary to tertiary care. Yet it seems that these cadres are not immune to the pressures toward increasing specialization and hospital concentration. In low-income countries, for example, the term "mid-level cadre" is more frequently associated with a more limited educational background and skill set, and the avoidance of qualifications that are internationally marketable appears to be a key characteristic. Nevertheless, such cadres have been demonstrated capable of substituting for medical and nursing staff in important health system roles.

The market also seems to fail to discipline private for-profit training schools—a growing feature in low- and middle-income countries (LMICs) particularly—in ways that ensure quality and production of graduates safe to practice their designated roles. The evidence on this issue is much weaker and restricted to one country case study each for medical and nursing education, with limited supporting evidence from other settings. Still, the convergence of the evidence from the Indian and Nepali case studies is striking, and as these two countries are relatively advanced in their private sector health professional training development, they are worthy of the attention of stakeholders in countries further back in the process.

Research Implications

Significant gaps in the evidence base emerge from the literature review. Research seeking to understand educational choice is dominated by the documentation of expressed rationales by students. These suffer from "social desirability bias" or the tendency of interviewees to give socially acceptable answers and may therefore overstate altruistic rationales for entry into health professions and subsequent training choices. More understanding of the characteristics of students choosing different paths is needed. The tendencies for students from rural backgrounds as more likely to take up rural practice and for students from lower socioeconomic backgrounds as more willing to take up community-based practice are quite well established in a number of contexts and suggest that more detailed research would have practical value for policy. Birenbaum-Carmeli (2002) and Birenbaum-Carivieli (2007) illustrate the type of analysis that may be capable of achieving greater understanding of not only the implications of different student recruitment strategies but also the potential to forecast emerging trends in student characteristics. These likely will have further implications for their choices beyond initial training and throughout their careers, hence relevant to the management of health workforce for 30–40 years.

There are parallels between excessive specialization in medical education and "professionalization" of nursing, yet the two processes are generally viewed differently. While increasingly high levels of nursing education have been shown to improve outcomes in hospital care, evidence at other levels is lacking, and more importantly, an overall analysis at the level of the health system as a whole has not been attempted, to our knowledge, in any country. This is at least in part because such an analysis represents a significant challenge. However, as with specialist medical education, it is insufficient to understand that specific health system roles are enhanced by such education: it is the overall availability and accessibility of competent health staff to meet the main health needs of the population that produces an affordable and effective health system, and it is only by this criterion that movements such as professionalization can be judged.

There is a similar absence of system-level evidence of the impact of the growing scope of mid-level providers, whether the nurse practitioner in the United States or the clinical officer in Kenya. Existing evidence is piecemeal, generally relates to small projects in which new cadres have been trained and their professional practice evaluated, and often suffers from the biases of positive-result publication and internal evaluation. The development of a new type of health professional has ramifications across a health system: by occupying space previously occupied by other cadres, for those cadres that might have domino effects across the health professional landscape, including for training curricula and for rates of return to education (RORE) in different health professions (which in some cases explains professional resistance to the introduction of new cadres).

Significant gaps were also identified in relation to private and social RORE. For the general education literature, it was suggested that the standard analysis overstates returns to primary education and understates returns to higher education potentially, resulting in substantial misallocation of public and international development assistance investments in education and providing potential explanation of the underinvestment in health professional education. For medical and nursing education in the United States, there was a reasonable body of evidence illustrating trends in private rates of return over time and the sensitivity of RORE estimates to methods of estimation and context (more so for medicine than nursing). Outside the United States, the literature search picked up very little evidence, limiting our understanding of the factors shaping health professional education choices, especially in LMICs.

Analysis of social rates of return to health professional education in general could be illustrated by a very small number of isolated studies. As with some other research gaps identified here, this can at least partially be explained by the complexity of the research task. In principle, social RORE encompass all stakeholders' perspectives and require an understanding of the effects of education on health outcomes. This is a tough challenge for analysis of specific roles, although research was identified that had estimated the impact of increasing nursing education for hospital outcomes, suggesting that while difficult, a larger picture of the social returns to specific educational investments at the system level may be an achievable research goal.

A better understanding of the *potential* social rates of return to health professional education would require further engagement with the production functions involved. Medical education in particular has been reported to be subject to significant cost inflation (at least in the United States), which might be explained by the growing body of knowledge required of a medical practitioner, likely to be reflected in the requirements of other health professionals. One study suggested shortening training as a means of reducing cost, but provided no evidence as to the impact of that proposal on quality of graduate or health outcomes. Very limited evidence was available on scale effects or other elements of production functions such as the implications of mixing faculty–student contact hours and other technologies including e-technologies. While there is an abundance of exposition of new technology in all educational areas, there were no studies we identified in relation to health professional education that evaluated these new possibilities in terms that could be translated into efficiency.

Evidence on the impact of growth of private sector health professional training institutions was recognized as severely limited. The accounts of the development of such institutions in medical training institutions in India and nurse training institutions in Nepal were fairly convincing, either because a number of reports were consistent (India) or because the single source resulted from rigorously conducted research (Nepal). Yet, wide gaps remain in the two accounts: for example, no objective assessment of quality standards of (public or private) training institutions was available, and as in other areas, the system-level impacts of the problems described have not been evaluated. No analysis was identified of the implications of quality deficits in training institutions for quality of practice in different health system roles and for health outcomes. As in other areas, this research is challenging but critically important.

In other countries where the private health professional education sector also appears to be growing rapidly—including Kenya, South Africa, and Thailand, where Reynolds et al. (2013) established an initial evidence base, as they also did for India—there is not even an adequate descriptive base of the phenomenon, and it will be important to establish this before more detailed analytic questions about the role played by private sector development can be addressed. For example, the Indian case study suggests that quality in the public sector may be affected by private sector development and this relationship is worthy of further study. The Indian and Nepali cases suggest that the market fails to discipline the health professional education sector, and while possible reasons for this are suggested for Nepal, how failures in the health care and capital markets, as well as other possible factors, conspire to produce important outcomes in health professional education is not understood.

Among the reasons for a weak research base with which to guide the questions addressed in this paper is a weak database in critical areas related to health education and labor markets. One reason for limited private RORE estimates outside the United States is the lack of data on wages and incomes of health professionals in other countries, and although the value of health professional data has become increasingly appreciated by governments and other key actors around the world, there are multiple problems with such data, as internationally reported.

For example, the common approach of reporting total numbers of each cadre does not capture the educational and training differences across countries nor actual workforce composition (Dieleman and Hilhorst 2011; Gupta, Castillo-Laborde, and Landry 2011; Gupta et al. 2011; Riley et al. 2012). The latter is important for differentiating the effect of provider education level on patient outcomes. For labor market analyses, the lack of data means incomplete predictions for actual market demands. Documentation of the size and distribution of health workforces in low-income countries has been improving, but even where heavy investments have been made in human resources for health (HRH) information systems, private sector employment tends to be poorly documented. Similarly, documentation of private training institutions and student numbers is often limited, as Adhikari (2010) found for Nepal. Much could be done to facilitate useful research in this area by setting up improved, routine data collection systems for key variables.

Policy Implications

Recognition of market forces' importance in determining the outcomes from health professional education systems implies the likely failure of planning and regulatory policies that ignore market forces. Examples of such policies include those that invest in training cadres of health workers deemed in shortage but that maintain unattractive pay and working conditions, leaving those trained hard to attract to empty posts, difficult to retain, and/or likely to seek further training to redirect their careers. It follows that if, as in many countries, there is a policy intention to rebalance the health system toward primary care, it is important that market signals as well as other factors align to support that intention.

Evidence from this paper suggests that in most settings they do not: differences in private RORE between specialist and primary care roles have tended to persist and even worsen with time and are clearly associated with career choices. Evidence from the United Kingdom's (possibly unintentional) experiment with a sharp increase in general practice pay suggests that where they do, a significant response is quickly forthcoming from students in favor of primary care roles.

Nevertheless, private RORE are determined by two variables: the private cost of education, and the value of future private returns. If it is deemed too expensive or difficult to change the balance of earnings streams toward primary care roles, there may be more scope than is generally recognized to change the balance of educational subsidy toward primary care roles. In educational policy debate, more generally, it is proposed that public subsidy be focused where public returns to education are highest, while students might be expected to fund their own education in areas where the returns are mostly private. Yet, countries generally do not distinguish between specialist and generalist training in allocating educational subsidy.

The paper has further implications for how public investments in education are directed. It seems that little attention has been paid to the cost-effectiveness or efficiency of health professional education. Policy makers could seek to encourage appropriate use of new technologies where it can improve on "chalk and talk" approaches. A key advantage of new technologies in contexts characterized by a history of weakness of educational systems is that the new generation becomes less dependent on the previous one for its access to learning opportunities. Considering scale efficiencies alongside other considerations about the concentration and distribution of educational opportunities might also enable higher output in quantity and/or quality terms from the same educational budget.

Other constraints to expanding publicly funded training opportunities other than public budgets have also been identified in the reviewed literature, including difficulties in recruiting and retaining adequate (quantity and quality) faculty. Ways of employing faculty members more efficiently may be identified, including through new technologies.

Another common difficulty appears to be assuring enough opportunities for students to gain practical experience through "placements" or "residency positions." The expansion of cadres and specialties focused on primary care, for which primary care rather than hospital experience is relevant and appropriate, increases the range of settings in which such experience can be gained, and there is now a growing experience of community-focused training schools and programs that demonstrate potential ways forward in both respects—in countries as diverse as Australia, the Philippines, and South Africa.

The pace of change in health care systems implies that the content and distribution of the training opportunities in (especially publicly subsidized) health professions require continuous reevaluation. Among the issues are those of specialization and professionalization. These are often driven from within the professions concerned, mediated through professional associations and colleges who accredit and recognize qualifications. The interests represented may be those of the professional groups themselves, looking to build their economic status and prestige, which may not align with a public policy focused on achieving universal health coverage (UHC), for example. Those making decisions about the investment of public resources need mechanisms that separate those decisions from the judgments of professional associations and colleges so that where there is conflict between interests, the priority for public investment is unequivocal.

This kind of conflict has been best recognized in developing new cadres. Although there is clearly potential for publication and internal evaluation biases, there is credible evidence of their cost-effectiveness in a range of contexts. This is likely to encourage further development of mid-level cadre roles involving investment in education. While research efforts seek to understand how this has impact at the level of the health system, policy makers will need to address several aspects: in what ways new cadres are substituting for old ones; in what ways they are complementing new ones; how teams need to be reconfigured; and with what implications for training numbers and curricula across the health professional training opportunities. This is complicated.

The review of evidence on private health professional training schools in LMICs highlights the difficulties of effective regulation. The Nepali case study suggests a scenario in which international shortage of health professionals has stoked demand for training vastly outstripping the public sector's capacity to finance it, and while this is less clearly the driving force of expansion of the private sector in India (likely to lie at least as much in India's growing internal demand), the implications appear similar. Regulations established when training school numbers are small may become impossible to implement as the phenomenon grows without greatly expanded regulatory infrastructure. Those with the most stake in improving regulation are the middle classes and foreign populations whom these health professionals will ultimately serve. Policy makers might look to those populations for support in resourcing improved regulation and, where relevant, tackling corruption in regulating institutions. Countries that do not yet have large private involvement in health professional training or entrenched problems in regulatory systems should learn from the experience of India and Nepal about the investment and safeguards required in the regulatory system.

The issues involved in managing and regulating markets in health professional education are challenging and often lack the evidence from which to build clear recommendations. A number of points are clear, however.

- Economic incentives are critically important in shaping demand for health professional training, routes taken through the stages of training, and the appropriateness of the emerging workforce for the public health needs of the population;
- Most countries manage economic incentives poorly with the result that the workforce is overspecialized and helps to shape an overmedicalized and hospital-centric system;
- Public investment in health professional training appears to miss opportunities to be more efficiently organized and effectively targeted in ways that could increase domestic production when appropriate;
- While the excess demand for health professional education and the need for health professionals make it tempting to liberalize training markets, there are important grounds for caution in encouraging the private sector to fill the gap.

APPENDIX A

Literature Search Strategy

Table A.1 Search Terms[a]

ENTRY BARRIER	NURS[a]	ASSIST[a]	PUBLIC
SPECIALTY CHOICE	DOCTOR	ROLE	PRIVATE
CAREER CHOICE	PHYSICIAN	EDUCAT[a]	
EDUCATION MARKET	DENT[a]	AUXIL[a]	
TRAINING SCHOOL	PHARMAC[a]	TECHNIC[a]	
VOCATIONAL TRAINING SCHOOL	MID(-)LEVEL		
TECHNICAL TRAINING SCHOOL	CLINICa		
BACHELOR TRAINING SCHOOL			
GRADUATE TRAINING SCHOOL			
POST(-)GRADUATE TRAINING SCHOOL			
RATE OF RETURN			
REGULATION			
EDUCATION QUALITY			
EDUCATION IMPACT			
CURRICULUM[a]			
HEALTH LABO(U)R MARKET			

a. Items in the same column were searched using the Boolean term "OR" or its equivalent and those in other columns using the Boolean term "AND." Mesh terms were searched in PubMed only.

Table A.2 MESH Terms

Higher-level heading	Subheading (not all available for all terms)
Nursing specialty	Economics
Medical specialty	Education
Career choice(s)	Manpower
Nursing education research	Supply and distribution
Nurse training school(s)	Statistics and numerical data
Education, professional	Trends
Nursing auxiliaries	

Coverage of the Literature in Relation to Private and Social Perspectives on the Rate of Return

Source	Country	Type of health professional training	Private cost	Social or public cost	Private return	Social or public return	Private rate of return	Social or public rate of return	Cost-benefit ratio
Adashi and Gruppuso (2010)	United States	Medicine	x						
Bicknell et al. (2001)	Vietnam	Medicine		x					
Hughes, Barker, and Reynolds (1991)	United States	Medicine	x						
Namate (1995)	Malawi	Nursing and midwifery	x	x					
Kerr and Brown (2006)	United States	Medicine	x		x		x		
Hader (2004)	United States	Nurse managers			x				
Kahn et al. (2006)	South Africa	General surgery			x				
Leigh et al. (2012)	United States	Medicine			x				
Luiz and Bahia (2009)	Brazil	Medicine			x				
McManus (2005)	UK	Medicine			x				
Nash and Brown (2012)	United States	Medicine			x				
Reschovsky and Staiti (2005)	United States	Medicine			x				
Siedenberg (1989)	United States	Nursing			x				
Simon, Dranove, and White (1998)	United States	Medicine			x				
Weeks and Wallace (2008)	United States	Medicine			x				
Weeks and Wallace (2002a)	United States	Medicine			x				
Burstein and Cromwell (1985)	United States	Medicine	x		x		x		
Cordes, Doherty, and Lopez (2001)	United States	Dentistry	x		x		x		
Cronin, Morgan, and Weeks (2010)	United States	Medicine	x		x		x		
Emery et al. (2006)	Canada	Medicine		x	x	x	x	x	
Fagerlund and Germano (2009)	United States	Nursing and midwifery	x	x	x	x	x	x	x

Source	Country	Type of health professional training	Private cost	Social or public cost	Private return	Social or public return	Private rate of return	Social or public rate of return	Cost-benefit ratio
Fagerlund (1998)	United States	Nurse anesthesia	x	x	x	x	x	x	x
Graf (2006)	United States	Nursing	x		x		x	x	
Hagemeier and Murawski (2011)	United States	Pharmacy	x		x		x		
Hartzema and Perfetto (1991)	United States	Pharmacy	x		x		x		
Langwell 1982	United States	Medicine	x		x		x		
Lapolla et al. (2004)	United States	Medicine		x		x		x	
Lowry (1992)	United States	Nursing	x		x		x		
Spetz and Bates (2013)	United States	Nursing	x		x		x		
Matthews et al. (2005)	United States	Pharmacy		x		x		x	
Mennemeyer (1978)	United States	Medicine	x		x		x		
		Pharmacy	x		x		x		
		Dentistry	x		x		x		
Mills et al (2011)	Africa	Medicine		x					
Mott and Kreling (1994)	United States	Pharmacy	x		x		x		
Newbold (2008)	United States	Nursing				x			
Pan and Straub (1997)	United States	Nursing	x		x		x		
Prashker and Meenan (1991)	United States	Medicine	x		x		x		
Schumacher (2011)	United States	Nursing			x				
Walker et al. (2002)	Indonesia	Midwifery		x		x			
Weeks et al. (1994)	United States	Medicine	x		x		x		
Weeks and Wallace (2002a, 2002b, 2002c)	United States	Medicine	x		x		x		

References

Adashi, Eli Y., and Philip A. Gruppuso. 2010. "Commentary: The Unsustainable Cost of Undergraduate Medical Education: An Overlooked Element of U.S. Health Care Reform." *Academic Medicine : Journal of the Association of American Medical Colleges* 85 (5): 763–65. doi:10.1097/ACM.0b013e3181d5cff7.

Bicknell, William J., Andrew C. Beggs, and Phi Van Tham. 2001. "Determining the Full Costs of Medical Education in Thai Binh, Vietnam: A Generalizable Model." *Health Policy and Planning* 16 (4) (December 1): 412–20. doi:10.1093/heapol/16.4.412.

Burstein, Philip L., and Jerry Cromwell. 1985. "Relative Incomes and Rates of Return for U.S. Physicians." *Journal of Health Economics* 4 (1) (March): 63–78.

Cordes, D. W., N. Doherty, and R. Lopez. 2001. "Assessing the Economic Return of Specializing in Orthodontics or Oral and Maxillofacial Surgery." *Journal of the American Dental Association (1939)* 132 (12) (December): 1679–84; quiz 1725–26.

Cronin, William A., Jessica A. Morgan, and William B. Weeks. 2010. "The Cost of Pursuing a Medical Career in the Military: A Tale of Five Specialties." *Academic Medicine : Journal of the Association of American Medical Colleges* 85 (8) (August): 1316–20. doi:10.1097/ACM.0b013e3181e5d6b8.

Emery, J. C. Herbert, Rodney A. Crutcher, Alexandra C. M. Harrison, and Howard Wright. 2006. "Social Rates of Return to Investment in Skills Assessment and Residency Training of International Medical Graduates in Alberta." *Health Policy* 79 (2–3) (December): 165–74. doi:10.1016/j.healthpol.2005.12.008.

Fagerlund, Kathleen A. 1998. "An Economic Analysis of the Investment in Nurse Anesthesia Education." *AANA Journal* 66 (2) (April): 153–60.

Fagerlund, Kathleen, and Elaine Germano. 2009. "The Costs and Benefits of Nurse-Midwifery Education: Model and Application." *Journal of Midwifery & Women's Health* 54 (5): 341–50. doi:10.1016/j.jmwh.2009.04.008.

Graf, Christina M. 2006. "ADN to BSN: Lessons from Human Capital Theory." *Nursing Economic* 24 (3): 135–41, 123; quiz 142.

Hader, Richard. 2004. "Salary Survey 2004. It's Time to Check Your Role's Return on Investment." *Nursing Management* 35 (7) (July): 28–32.

Hagemeier, Nicholas E., and Matthew M. Murawski. 2011. "Economic Analysis of Earning a PhD Degree after Completion of a PharmD Degree." *American Journal of Pharmaceutical Education* 75 (1): 15. doi:10.5688/ajpe75115.

Hartzema, A. G., and E. Perfetto. 1991. "Pharmaceutical Sciences' Manpower Supply and Internal Rate of Return." *Pharmaceutical Research* 8 (6): 676–82.

Hughes, R. G., D. C. Barker, and R. C. Reynolds. 1991. "Are We Mortgaging the Medical Profession?" *The New England Journal of Medicine* 325 (6): 404–07. doi:10.1056/nejm199108083250606.

Kahn, D., S. Pillay, M. G. Veller, E. Panieri, and M. J. R. Westcott. 2006. "General Surgery in Crisis—the Critical Shortage." *South African Journal of Surgery. Suid-Afrikaanse Tydskrif Vir Chirurgie* 44 (3): 88–92, 94.

Kerr, Jason R., and Jeffrey J. Brown. 2006. "Costs of a Medical Education: Comparison with Graduate Education in Law and Business." *JACR Journal of the American College of Radiology*. doi:10.1016/j.jacr.2005.09.010.

Langwell, K. M. 1982. "Differences by Sex in Economic Returns Associated with Physician Specialization." *Journal of Health Politics, Policy and Law* 6: 752–61. doi:10.1215/03616878-6-4-752.

Lapolla, Michael, Edward N. Brandt, Andréa Barker, and Lori Ryan. 2004. "The Economic Impacts of Oklahoma's Family Medicine Residency Programs." *The Journal of the Oklahoma State Medical Association* 97 (6) (June): 248–51.

Leigh, J. Paul, Daniel Tancredi, Anthony Jerant, Patrick S. Romano, and Richard L. Kravitz. 2012. "Lifetime Earnings for Physicians across Specialties." *Medical Care* 50 (12) (December): 1. doi:10.1097/MLR.0b013e318268ac0c.

Lowry, L. W. 1992. "Is a Baccalaureate in Nursing Worth It?" *Nursing Economic* 10 (1): 46–52.

Luiz, Ronir Raggio, and Lígia Bahia. 2009. "Income and Vocational Integration of Brazilian Physicians since the Establishment of the National Health System." *Revista de Saude Publica* 43 (4): 689–98.

Matthews, Jamie, Mark Pingle, Robert Sullivan, Paul Ferguson, James E. Rogers, and Iain L. O. Buxton. 2005. "Economic Justification for a Public School of Pharmacy: Lessons for Nevada." *Proceedings of the Western Pharmacology Society* 48: 1–12.

McManus, I. C. 2005. "The Wealth of Distinguished Doctors: Retrospective Survey." *BMJ (Clinical Research Ed.)* 331 (7531) (December 24): 1520–23. doi:10.1136/bmj.331.7531.1520.

Mennemeyer, S. T. 1978. "Really Great Returns to Medical Education?" *The Journal of Human Resources* 13 (1) (January): 75–90.

Mills, Edward J., Steve Kanters, Amy Hagopian, Nick Bansback, Jean Nachega, Mark Alberton, Christopher G. Au-Yeung, et al. 2011. "The Financial Cost of Doctors Emigrating from Sub-Saharan Africa: Human Capital Analysis." *BMJ* 343: d7031. doi:10.1136/bmj.d7031.

Mott, D. A., and D. H. Kreling. 1994. "An Internal Rate of Return Approach to Investigate Pharmacist Supply in the United States." *Health Economics* 3 (6): 373–84.

Namate, Dorothy E. 1995. "The Cost of Registered Nurse-Midwifery Education in Malawi." *Journal of Advanced Nursing* 22 (3): 410–15. doi:10.1046/j.1365-2648.1995.22030410.x.

Nash, Kent D., and L. Jackson Brown. 2012. "The Structure and Economics of Dental Education." *Journal of Dental Education* 76 (8) (August 1): 987–95.

Newbold, David. 2008. "The Production Economics of Nursing: A Discussion Paper." *International Journal of Nursing Studies* 45 (1): 120–28. doi:10.1016/j.ijnurstu.2007.01.007.

Pan, S., and L. Straub. 1997. "Returns to Nursing Education: Rural and Nonrural Practice." *The Journal of Rural Health : Official Journal of the American Rural Health Association and the National Rural Health Care Association* 13 (1) (January): 78–85. doi:10.1111/j.1748-0361.1997.tb00836.x.

Prashker, M. J., and R. F. Meenan. 1991. "Subspecialty Training: Is It Financially Worthwhile?" *Annals of Internal Medicine* 115 (9) (November 1): 715–19.

Reschovsky, James D., and Andrea B. Staiti. 2005. "Physician Incomes in Rural and Urban America." *Issue Brief (Center for Studying Health System Change)* 92: 1–4.

Schumacher, Edward J. 2011. "Foreign-Born Nurses in the US Labor Market." *Health Economics* 20 (3): 362–78. doi:10.1002/hec.1595.

Siedenberg, J. M. 1989. "Investing in Nursing Education: Some Evidence of Immediate Private Monetary Benefits." *The Journal of Nursing Education* 28 (5): 210–14.

Simon, Carol J., David Dranove, and William D. White. 1998. "The Effect of Managed Care on the Incomes of Primary Care and Specialty Physicians." *Health Services Research* 33 (3 Pt 1): 549–69.

Spetz, Joanne, and Timothy Bates. 2013. "Is a Baccalaureate in Nursing Worth It? The Return to Education, 2000–2008." *Health Services Research* 48 (6 PART1) (December): 1859–78. doi:10.1111/1475-6773.12104.

Walker, Damian, Jeanne M. McDermott, Julia Fox-Rushby, Marwan Tanjung, Mardiati Nadjib, Dono Widiatmoko, and Endang Achadi. 2002. "An Economic Analysis of Midwifery Training Programmes in South Kalimantan, Indonesia." *Bulletin of the World Health Organization* 80 (1): 47–55. doi:S0042-96862002000100009 [pii].

Weeks, William B., and Amy E. Wallace. 2002a. "Medicare Payment Changes and Physicians' Incomes." *Journal of Health Care Finance* 29 (2) (January): 18–26.

———. 2002b. "The More Things Change: Revisiting a Comparison of Educational Costs and Incomes of Physicians and Other Professionals." *Academic Medicine : Journal of the Association of American Medical Colleges* 77 (4) (April): 312–19.

———. 2002c. "Long-Term Financial Implications of Specialty Training for Physicians." *The American Journal of Medicine* 113 (5) (October 1): 393–9.

Weeks, William B., Amy E. Wallace, Myron M. Wallace, and H. Gilbert. Welch. 1994. "A Comparison of the Educational Costs and Incomes of Physicians and Other Professionals." *The New England Journal of Medicine* 330 (18) (May 5): 1280–86. doi:10.1097/00132586-199412000-00060.

Weeks, William B., and Tanner A. Wallace. 2008. "Medical School Type and Physician Income." *Journal of Health Care Finance* 34 (3) (January): 34–44.

Estimates of Private Rates of Return and Net Present Value

First author and date of publication	Country	Education program	Date of estimate	Estimate (annual rate of return unless otherwise stated)
Sloan (1968)[a]	United States	Medicine	1962 1966	16.6% 18.2%
Fein and Weber (1971)[a]	United States	Medicine	1966	15%
Feldman and Scheffler (1978)[a]	United States	Medicine	1970	22%
Mennemeyer (1978)	United States	Medicine compared to dentistry, pharmacy, and other professions		NPV @ 10% discount rate $10,876 compared to dentistry $49,491 compared to pharmacy NPV @4% discount rate $66,362 compared to dentistry $182,197 compared to pharmacy
Burstein and Cromwell (1985)	United States	Medicine	1980	14–17%
Langwell (1982)	United States	Medicine		
Prashker and Meenan (1991)	United States	Medicine (Rheumatology compared to gastroenterology)		NPV @5% $1,101,863 lower NPV @ 10% $512,952 lower
Weeks et al. (1994)	United States	Medicine	1990	'Procedure based medicine': 20.23% 'Primary care medicine': 15.28%
Weeks and Wallace (2002b)	United States	Medicine	1997	'Procedure based medicine': 18% 'Primary care medicine': 16%

table continues next page

First author and date of publication	Country	Education program	Date of estimate	Estimate (annual rate of return unless otherwise stated)
Weeks and Wallace (2002a, 2002c)	United States	Medicine	1992 1998	General surgery 28% Orthopedics 47% Urology 39% Otolaryngology 36% Opthalmology 34% Primary care 15% General surgery 16% Orthopedics 27% Urology 25% Otolaryngology 11% Opthalmology 13% Primary care 3%
Lowry (1992)	United States	Baccalaureate nursing degree compared to diploma and associate degree		NPV × 4 compared to diploma NPV × 3 compared to associate degree
Fagerlund (1998)	United States	Nurse anesthesia		23%
Pan and Straub (1997)	United States	Nursing		Return to rural practice generally lower than return to urban practice
Graf (2006)	United States	Baccalaureate nursing degree compared to associate degree		−5.5%
Fagerlund and Germano (2009)	United States	Nursing and midwifery		11.5%
Hartzema and Perfetto (1991)	United States	Pharmacy		In academic career: 16% In pharmaceutical industry: 8.1% (81%?)
Mott and Kreling (1994)	United States	Pharmacy	1983 1985 1987 1989 1991	9.4% 8.94% 9.96% 12.25% 14.58%
Hageimeier and Murawski (2011)	United States	PhD for pharmacists		−1.4 – −1.3% Negative trend

Note: Positive net present values (NPVs) imply rates of return higher than the discount rate applied. All estimates are for the United States. Most are for medicine, either overall or comparing across specialties. The dates of estimates are highly divergent. No effort has been made to adjust reported NPVs to a common price level.

a. Cited by Roth 2011.

References

Burstein, Philip L., and Jerry Cromwell. 1985. "Relative Incomes and Rates of Return for U.S. Physicians." *Journal of Health Economics* 4 (1) (March): 63–78.

Fagerlund, Kathleen A. 1998. "An Economic Analysis of the Investment in Nurse Anesthesia Education." *AANA Journal* 66 (2) (April): 153–60.

Fagerlund, Kathleen, and Elaine Germano. 2009. "The Costs and Benefits of Nurse-Midwifery Education: Model and Application." *Journal of Midwifery & Women's Health* 54 (5): 341–50. doi:10.1016/j.jmwh.2009.04.008.

Fein, Rashi, and Gerald Weber. 1971. *Financing Medical Education*. New York, New York: Carnegie Commission on Higher Education. 245–53.

Feldman, R., and R. Scheffler. 1978. "The Supply of Medical School Applicants and the Rate of Return to Training." *Quarterly Review of Economics and Business* 82: 91–98.

Graf, Christina M. 2006. "ADN to BSN: Lessons from Human Capital Theory." *Nursing Economic* 24 (3): 135–41, 123; quiz 142.

Hagemeier, Nicholas E., and Matthew M. Murawski. 2011. "Economic Analysis of Earning a PhD Degree after Completion of a PharmD Degree." *American Journal of Pharmaceutical Education* 75 (1): 15. doi:10.5688/ajpe75115.

Hartzema, A. G., and E. Perfetto. 1991. "Pharmaceutical Sciences' Manpower Supply and Internal Rate of Return." *Pharmaceutical Research* 8 (6): 676–82.

Langwell, K. M. 1982. "Differences by Sex in Economic Returns Associated with Physician Specialization." *Journal of Health Politics, Policy and Law* 6: 752–61. doi:10.1215/03616878–6–4–752.

Lowry, L. W. 1992. "Is a Baccalaureate in Nursing Worth It?" *Nursing Economic* 10 (1): 46–52.

Mennemeyer, S. T. 1978. "Really Great Returns to Medical Education?" *The Journal of Human Resources* 13 (1) (January): 75–90.

Mott, D. A., and D. H. Kreling. 1994. "An Internal Rate of Return Approach to Investigate Pharmacist Supply in the United States." *Health Economics* 3 (6): 373–84.

Pan, S., and L. Straub. 1997. "Returns to Nursing Education: Rural and Nonrural Practice." *The Journal of Rural Health : Official Journal of the American Rural Health Association and the National Rural Health Care Association* 13 (1) (January): 78–85. doi:10.1111/j.1748-0361.1997.tb00836.x.

Prashker, M. J., and R. F. Meenan. 1991. "Subspecialty Training: Is It Financially Worthwhile?" *Annals of Internal Medicine* 115 (9) (November 1): 715–19.

Roth, N. 2011. *The Costs and Returns to Medical Education*. https://elsa.berkeley.edu/econ/ugrad/theses/roth_nicholas.pdf.

Sloan, Frank A. 1968. Economic Models of Physician Supply. Doctoral dissertation. Harvard University.

Weeks, William B., and Amy E. Wallace. 2002a. "Medicare Payment Changes and Physicians' Incomes." *Journal of Health Care Finance* 29 (2) (January): 18–26.

———. 2002b. "The More Things Change: Revisiting a Comparison of Educational Costs and Incomes of Physicians and Other Professionals." *Academic Medicine : Journal of the Association of American Medical Colleges* 77 (4) (April): 312–19.

———. 2002c. "Long-Term Financial Implications of Specialty Training for Physicians." *The American Journal of Medicine* 113 (5) (October 1): 393–99.

Weeks, William B., Amy E. Wallace, Myron M. Wallace, and H. Gilbert. Welch. 1994. "A Comparison of the Educational Costs and Incomes of Physicians and Other Professionals." *The New England Journal of Medicine* 330 (18) (May 5): 1280–86. doi:10.1097/00132586–199412000–00060.

References

Abbott, Andrew. 1988. *The System of Professions*. 1st ed. Chicago: University of Chicago Press.

Abdul Hamid, A. K. 2000. "Private Medical Education—the Doctor's Perspective." *Medical Journal of Malaysia* 55 (Suppl B) (August): 23–27.

Abendroth, Jens, Ute Schnell, Thomas Lichte, Matthias Oemler, and Andreas Klement. 2014. "Motives of Former Interns in General Practice for Speciality-Choice—Results of a Cross-Sectional Study among Graduates 2007 to 2012." *German Journal for Medical Education* 31 (1): Doc11. doi:10.3205/zma000903.

Adhikari, R. 2010. "From Aspirations to Dream Trap". Nurse Education in Nepal and Nepali Nurse Migration to the UK. University of Edinburgh.

Agency for Healthcare Research and Quality. 2014. "2013 National Healthcare Disparities Report (NHDR)." Washington, DC.

Aiken, Linda H., Ying Xue, Sean P. Clarke, and Douglas M. Sloane. 2007. "Supplemental Nurse Staffing in Hospitals and Quality of Care." *The Journal of Nursing Administration* 37 (7–8): 335–42.

Akerlof, George A. 1970. "The Market for 'Lemons': Quality Uncertainty and the Market Mechanism." *The Quarterly Journal of Economics* 84 (3): 488–500.

Al-Dlaigan, Yousef H., Ra'ed Al-Sadhan, Mohammed Al-Ghamdi, Abdullah Al-Shahrani, and Mohammed Al-Shahrani. 2011. "Postgraduate Specialties Interest, Career Choices and Qualifications Earned by Male Dentists Graduated from King Saud University." *Saudi Dental Journal* 23 (2) (April): 81–86. doi:10.1016/j.sdentj.2010.11.004.

Almeida-Filho, Naomar. 2011. "Higher Education and Health Care in Brazil." *Lancet* 377: 1898–1900. doi:10.1016/S0140-6736(11)60326-7.

Ananthakrishnan, N. 2007. "The Entrance Examination Fiasco in Tamil Nadu." *National Medical Journal of India* 20 (3): 160.

———. 2010. "Medical Education in India: Is It Still Possible to Reverse the Downhill Trend?" *National Medical Journal of India* 23 (3): 156–60.

Ananthakrishnan, N., and A. K. Shanthi. 2012. "Attempts at Regulation of Medical Education by the MCI: Issues of Unethical and Dubious Practices for Compliance by Medical Colleges and Some Possible Solutions." *Indian Journal of Medical Ethics* 9 (1): 37–42.

Aslam, M., A. Ali, T. Taj, N. Badar, W. Mirza, A. Ammar, S. Muzaffar, and J. R. Kauten. 2011. "Specialty Choices of Medical Students and House Officers in Karachi, Pakistan." *Eastern Mediterranean Health Journal = La Revue de Sante de La Mediterranee Orientale = Al-Majallah Al-Sihhiyah Li-Sharq Al-Mutawassit* 17 (1): 74–79.

Atchison, Kathryn A., Ronald S. Mito, Dara Jean Rosenberg, Karen H. Lefever, Sylvia Lin, and Rita Engelhardt. 2002. "PGD Training and Its Impact on General Dentist Practice Patterns." *Journal of Dental Education* 66 (12): 1348–57.

Auerbach, David I., Peter I. Buerhaus, and Douglas O. Staiger. 2011. "Registered Nurse Supply Grows Faster than Projected amid Surge in New Entrants Ages 23–26." *Health Affairs (Project Hope)* 30 (12) (December): 2286–92. doi:10.1377/hlthaff.2011.0588.

Ayandiran, Emmanuel Olufemi, Omolola Oladunni Irinoye, Joel Olayiwola Faronbi, and Ntombe G. Mtshali. 2013. "Education Reforms in Nigeria: How Responsive Is the Nursing Profession?" *International Journal of Nursing Education Scholarship* 10 (16). doi:10.1515/ijnes-2012-0016.

Bach, Stephen. 2007. "Going Global? The Regulation of Nurse Migration in the UK." *British Journal of Industrial Relations* 45 (2) (June): 383–03.

Bailey, Nicola, Kate L. Mandeville, Tim Rhodes, Mwapatsa Mipando, and Adamson S. Muula. 2012. "Postgraduate Career Intentions of Medical Students and Recent Graduates in Malawi: A Qualitative Interview Study." *BMC Medical Education* 12 (January): 87. doi:10.1186/1472–6920–12–87.

Bicknell, William J., Andrew C. Beggs, and Phi Van Tham. 2001. "Determining the Full Costs of Medical Education in Thai Binh, Vietnam: A Generalizable Model." *Health Policy and Planning* 16 (4) (December 1): 412–20. doi:10.1093/heapol/16.4.412.

Birenbaum-Carivieli, Daphna. 2007. "Contextualizing Nurse Education in Israel: Sociodemography, Labor Market Dynamics and Professional Training." *Contemporary Nurse : A Journal for the Australian Nursing Profession* 24 (2) (April): 117–27. doi:10.5172/conu.2007.24.2.117.

Birenbaum-Carmeli, Daphna. 2002. "Nurse Education and the Labour Market: An Israeli Case Study." *Nurse Education Today* 22 (7) (October): 563–70. doi:10.1054/nedt.2002.0777.

Bittaye, Mustapha, Akin-Tunde Ademola Odukogbe, Ousman Nyan, Bintou Jallow, and Akinyinka O. Omigbodun. 2012. "Medical Students' Choices of Specialty in The Gambia: The Need for Career Counseling." *BMC Medical Education* 12 (January): 72. doi:10.1186/1472–6920–12–72.

Blaauw, Duane, Prudence Ditlopo, Fresier Maseko, Maureen Chirwa, Aziza Mwisongo, Posy Bidwell, Steve Thomas, and Charles Normand. 2013. "Comparing the Job Satisfaction and Intention to Leave of Different Categories of Health Workers in Tanzania, Malawi, and South Africa." *Global Health Action* 6 (January): 19287.

Bland, Carole J., Linda N. Meurer, and George Maldonado. 1995. "Determinants of Primary Care Specialty Choice: A Non-Statistical Meta-Analysis of the Literature." *Academic Medicine : Journal of the Association of American Medical Colleges* 70 (7) (July): 620–41.

Blaug, Mark. 1968. *An Introduction to the Economics of Education*. 1st ed. London: Penguin.

Bodenheimer, Thomas, Robert A. Berenson, and Paul Rudolf. 2007. "The Primary Care-Specialty Income Gap: Why It Matters." *Annals of Internal Medicine* 146 (4) (February 20): 301–06.

Brotherton, Sarah E., and Sylvia I. Etzel. 2007. "Graduate Medical Education 2006–2007." *Journal of the American Medical Association* 298 (9): 1081–96.

———. 2013. "Graduate Medical Education, 2012–13." *Journal of the American Medical Association* 310 (21): 2328–46.

Buchan, James, Fiona O'May, and Gilles Dussault. 2013. "Nursing Workforce Policy and the Economic Crisis: A Global Overview." *Journal of Nursing Scholarship* 45 (3): 298–307.

Buerhaus, Peter I., David I. Auerbach, and Douglas O. Staiger. 2007. "Recent Trends in the Registered Nurse Labor Market in the U.S.: Short-Run Swings on Top of Long-Term Trends." *Nursing Economic$* 25 (2): 59–66, 55; quiz 67.

Burch, V. C., D. McKinley, J. van Wyk, S. Kiguli-Walube, D. Cameron, F. J. Cilliers, A. O. Longombe, C. Mkony, C. Okoromah, B. Otieno-Nyunya, and P. S. Morahan. 2011. "Career Intentions of Medical Students Trained in Six Sub-Saharan African Countries." *Education for Health (Abingdon, England)* 24 (3): 614.

Burstein, Philip L., and Jerry Cromwell. 1985. "Relative Incomes and Rates of Return for U.S. Physicians." *Journal of Health Economics* 4 (1) (March): 63–78.

Chew, Yu Wei, Sudeash Rajakrishnan, Chin Aun Low, Prakash Kumar Jayapalan, and Chandrashekhar T. Sreeramareddy. 2011. "Medical Students' Choice of Specialty and Factors Determining Their Choice: A Cross-Sectional Questionnaire Survey in Melaka-Manipal Medical College, Malaysia." *BioScience Trends* 5 (2): 69–76. doi:10.5582/bst.2011.v5.2.69.

Choy, Catherine Ceniza. 2006. *Empire of Care*. 1st ed. Durham, NC: Duke University Press.

Couper, Ian D., and Paul S. Worley. 2010. "Meeting the Challenges of Training More Medical Students: Lessons from Flinders University's Distributed Medical Education Program." *The Medical Journal of Australia* 193 (1) (July 5): 34–36.

Creed, Peter A., Judy Searle, and Mary E. Rogers. 2010. "Medical Specialty Prestige and Lifestyle Preferences for Medical Students." *Social Science and Medicine* 71 (6) (September): 1084–88. doi:10.1016/j.socscimed.2010.06.027.

Cristobal, F., and P. Worley. 2012. "Can Medical Education in Poor Rural Areas Be Costeffective and Sustainable: The Case of the Ateneo de Zamboanga University School of Medicine." *Rural and Remote Health* 12: 1835.

Das, Anindya. 2012. "Medical PG Seats Being Sold! The Conundrum of Privatized Medical Education." *The Indian Journal of Medical Research* 135 (January): 255–57.

DeMaria, Lisa M., Lourdes Campero, Marianne Vidler, and Dilys Walker. 2012. "Non-Physician Providers of Obstetric Care in Mexico: Perspectives of Physicians, Obstetric Nurses and Professional Midwives." *Human Resources for Health*. doi:10.1186/1478-4491-10-6.

Department of Health and Human Services. 2005. "Nursing Education in Five States: The Importance of State Appropriations to Sustain Nursing School Capacity in States with Acute Nurse Shortages." Washington, DC.

DeZee, Kent J., Douglas Maurer, Ross Colt, William Shimeall, Renee Mallory, John Powers, and Steven J. Durning. 2011. "Effect of Financial Remuneration on Specialty Choice of Fourth-Year U.S. Medical Students." *Academic Medicine : Journal of the Association of American Medical Colleges* 86 (2): 187–93. doi:10.1097/ACM.0b013e3182045ec9.

Dhima, Matilda, Vicki C. Petropoulos, Rita K. Han, Taru Kinnunen, and Robert F. Wright. 2012. "Dental Students' Perceptions of Dental Specialties and Factors Influencing Specialty and Career Choices." *Journal of Dental Education* 76: 562–73. doi:76/5/562 [pii].

Dicicco-Bloom, Barbara. 2004. "The Racial and Gendered Experiences of Immigrant Nurses from Kerala, India." *Journal of Transcultural Nursing : Official Journal of the*

Transcultural Nursing Society/Transcultural Nursing Society 15 (1) (January): 26–33. doi:10.1177/1043659603260029.

Dickson, Matt, and Colm Harmon. 2011. "Economic Returns to Education: What We Know, What We Don't Know, and Where We Are Going-Some Brief Pointers." *Economics of Education Review* 30 (6): 1118–22. doi:10.1016/j.econedurev.2011.08.003.

Dieleman, Marjolein, and Thea Hilhorst. 2011. "Governance and Human Resources for Health." *Human Resources for Health* 9 (1) (January): 29. doi:10.1186/1478–4491-9-29.

Diwan, Vishal, Christie Minj, Neeraj Chhari, and Ayesha De Costa. 2013. "Indian Medical Students in Public and Private Sector Medical Schools: Are Motivations and Career Aspirations Different? — Studies from Madhya Pradesh, India." *BMC Medical Education* 13 (1) (January): 127. doi:10.1186/1472–6920-13-127.

Doroghazi, Robert M., and Joseph S. Alpert. 2014. "A Medical Education as an Investment: Financial Food for Thought." *American Journal of Medicine*. doi:10.1016/j.amjmed.2013.08.004.

Dos Santos, Beatriz F., Belinda Nicolau, Katia Muller, Christophe Bedos, and Angela Cristina Cilense-Zuanon. 2013. "Brazilian Dental Students' Intentions and Motivations towards Their Professional Career." *Journal of Dental Education* 77 (3): 337–44.

Dovlo, Delanyo. 2007. "Migration of Nurses from Sub-Saharan Africa: A Review of Issues and Challenges." *Health Services Research*. doi:10.1111/j.1475-6773.2007.00712.x.

Dower, Catherine, Jean Moore, and Margaret Langelier. 2013. "Analysis & Commentary: It Is Time to Restructure Health Professions Scope-of-Practice Regulations to Remove Barriers to Care." *Health Affairs* 32 (11) (November): 1971–76. doi:10.1377/hlthaff.2013.0537.

Drevdahl, Denise J., and Kathleen Shannon Dorcy. 2007. "Exclusive Inclusion: The Violation of Human Rights and US Immigration Policy." *Advances in Nursing Science* 30 (4): 290–302. doi:10.1097/01.ANS.0000300179.64101.81.

Dubowitz, Gerald, Sarah Detlefs, and Kelley A. McQueen. 2010. "Global Anesthesia Workforce Crisis: A Preliminary Survey Revealing Shortages Contributing to Undesirable Outcomes and Unsafe Practices." *World Journal of Surgery* 34 (3): 438–44. doi:10.1007/s00268-009-0229-6.

Eastaugh, S. R. 1985. "The Impact of the Nurse Training Act on the Supply of Nurses, 1974–1983." *Inquiry* 22 (4): 404–17.

Emery, J. C. Herbert, Rodney A. Crutcher, Alexandra C. M. Harrison, and Howard Wright. 2006. "Social Rates of Return to Investment in Skills Assessment and Residency Training of International Medical Graduates in Alberta." *Health Policy* 79 (2–3) (December): 165–74. doi:10.1016/j.healthpol.2005.12.008.

Erikson, Clese E., Sana Danish, Karen C. Jones, Shana F. Sandberg, and Adam C. Carle. 2013. "The Role of Medical School Culture in Primary Care Career Choice." *Academic Medicine* 88 (12): 1919–26. doi:10.1097/acm.0000000000000038.

Evans, Julie, Trevor Lambert, and Michael Goldacre. 2002. "GP Recruitment and Retention: A Qualitative Analysis of Doctors' Comments about Training for and Working in General Practice." *Occasional Paper (Royal College of General Practitioners)* (83) (February): iii–vi, 1–33.

Foreman, Spencer. 1996. "Managing the Physician Workforce: Hands Off, the Market Is Working." *Health Affairs (Project Hope)* 15 (2): 243–49. doi:10.1377/hlthaff.15.2.243.

Freidson, Eliot. 1970. *Professional Dominance*. 1st ed. New York: Atherton Press, Inc.

Freire, Maria do Carmo Matias, Lidia Moraes Ribeiro Jordao, Naiara de Paula Ferreira, Maria de Fatima Nunes, Maria Goretti Queiroz, and Claudio Rodrigues Leles. 2011. "Motivation towards Career Choice of Brazilian Freshman Students in a Fifteen-Year Period." *Journal of Dental Education* 75 (1): 115–21. doi:75/1/115 [pii].

Frenk, Julio, Lincoln Chen, Zulfiqar A. Bhutta, Jordan Cohen, Nigel Crisp, Timothy Evans, Harvey Fineberg, Patricia Garcia, Yang Ke, Patrick Kelley, Barry Kistnasamy, Afaf Meleis, David Naylor, Ariel Pablos-Mendez, Srinath Reddy, Susan Scrimshaw, Jaime Sepulveda, David Serwadda, and Huda Zurayk. 2010. "Health Professionals for a New Century: Transforming Education to Strengthen Health Systems in an Interdependent World." *Lancet* 376 (9756) (December 4): 1923–58. doi:10.1016/S0140–6736(10)61854–5.

Fulton, Brent D., Richard M. Scheffler, Susan P. Sparkes, Erica Yoonkyung Auh, Marko Vujicic, and Agnes Soucat. 2011. "Health Workforce Skill Mix and Task Shifting in Low Income Countries: A Review of Recent Evidence." *Human Resources for Health* 9 (1) (January): 1. doi:10.1186/1478–4491–9–1.

Gagné, Robert, and Pierre Thomas Léger. 2005. "Determinants of Physicians' Decisions to Specialize." *Health Economics* 14 (7): 721–35. doi:10.1002/hec.970.

Gallagher, Jennifer E., Wendy Clarke, and Nairn H. F. Wilson. 2008. "The Emerging Dental Workforce: Short-Term Expectations Of, and Influences on Dental Students Graduating from a London Dental School in 2005." *Primary Dental Care : Journal of the Faculty of General Dental Practitioners (UK)* 15 (3): 93–101. doi:10.1308/135576108784795392.

George, Gavin, Jeff Gow, and Shaneel Bachoo. 2013. "Understanding the Factors Influencing Health-Worker Employment Decisions in South Africa." *Human Resources for Health* 11 (1) (January): 15. doi:10.1186/1478–4491–11–15.

Gibis, Bernhard, Andreas Heinz, Rüdiger Jacob, and Carl-Heinz Müller. 2012. "The Career Expectations of Medical Students: Findings of a Nationwide Survey in Germany." *Deutsches Ärzteblatt International* 109 (18) (May): 327–32. doi:10.3238/arztebl.2012.0327.

Gill, Harbir, Scott McLeod, Kimberley Duerksen, and Olga Szafran. 2012. "Factors Influencing Medical Students' Choice of Family Medicine: Effects of Rural versus Urban Background." *Canadian Family Physician* 58 (11): e649–57.

González-Robledo, Luz Maria, Maria Cecilia González-Robledo, and Gustavo Nigenda. 2012. "Dentist Education and Labour Market in Mexico:elements for Policy Definition." *Human Resources for Health* 10 (1) (January): 31. doi:10.1186/1478–4491–10–31.

González-Torrente, Susana, Jordi Pericas-Beltrán, Miguel Bennasar-Veny, Rosa Adrover-Barceló, José M. Morales-Asencio, and Joan De Pedro-Gómez. 2012. "Perception of Evidence-Based Practice and the Professional Environment of Primary Health Care Nurses in the Spanish Context: A Cross-Sectional Study." *BMC Health Services Research* 12 (1): 227. doi:10.1186/1472–6963–12–227.

Gouthro, Trina Johnena. 2009. "Recognizing and Addressing the Stigma Associated with Mental Health Nursing: A Critical Perspective." *Issues in Mental Health Nursing* 30 (11): 669–76. doi:10.3109/01612840903040274.

Gowin, Ewelina, Wanda Horst-Sikorska, Michal Michalak, Dirk Avonts, Krzysztof Buczkowski, Witold Lukas, Tomasz Korman, Aalicja Litwiejko, and Slawomir Chlabicz. 2014. "The Attractiveness of Family Medicine among Polish Medical

Students." *European Journal of General Practice* 20 (2): 121–24. doi:10.3109/1381478
8.2013.826643.

Gragnolati, Michele, Magnus Lindelow, and Bernard Couttolenc. 2013. *Twenty Years of Health System Reform in Brazil.* Directions in Development. Washington, DC: World Bank. doi:10.1596/978-0-8213-9843-2.

Gupta, Neeru, Blerta Maliqi, Adson França, Frank Nyonator, Muhammad A. Pate, David Sanders, Hedia Belhadj, and Bernadette Daelmans. 2011. "Human Resources for Maternal, Newborn and Child Health: From Measurement and Planning to Performance for Improved Health Outcomes." *Human Resources for Health* 9 (1) (January): 16. doi:10.1186/1478-4491-9-16.

Gupta, Neeru, Carla Castillo-Laborde, and Michel D. Landry. 2011. "Health-Related Rehabilitation Services: Assessing the Global Supply of and Need for Human Resources." *BMC Health Services Research.* doi:10.1186/1472-6963-11-276.

Hagemeier, Nicholas E., and Matthew M. Murawski. 2011. "Economic Analysis of Earning a PhD Degree after Completion of a PharmD Degree." *American Journal of Pharmaceutical Education* 75 (1): 15. doi:10.5688/ajpe75115.

Hagopian, Amy, Anthony Ofosu, Adesegun Fatusi, Richard Biritwum, Ama Essel, L. Gary Hart, and Carolyn Watts. 2005. "The Flight of Physicians from West Africa: Views of African Physicians and Implications for Policy." *Social Science and Medicine.* doi:10.1016/j.socscimed.2005.03.027.

Halter, Mary, Vari Drennan, Kaushik Chattopadhyay, Wilfred Carneiro, Jennifer Yiallouros, Simon de Lusignan, Heather Gage, Jonathan Gabe, and Robert Grant. 2013. "The Contribution of Physician Assistants in Primary Care: A Systematic Review." *BMC Health Services Research* 13 (1) (January): 223. doi:10.1186/1472-6963-13-223.

Hanrahan, Nancy P. 2007. "Measuring Inpatient Psychiatric Environments: Psychometric Properties of the Practice Environment Scale-Nursing Work Index (PES-NWI)." *International Journal of Psychiatric Nursing Research* 12 (3): 1521–28.

Happell, Brenda, and Cadeyrn J. Gaskin. 2013. "The Attitudes of Undergraduate Nursing Students towards Mental Health Nursing: A Systematic Review." *Journal of Clinical Nursing.* doi:10.1111/jocn.12022.

Harvey, Adrian, Jean Gaston DesCôteaux, and Sandra Banner. 2005. "Trends in Disciplines Selected by Applicants in the Canadian Resident Matches, 1994–2004." *CMAJ* 172 (6) (March 15): 737. doi:10.1503/cmaj.1040146.

Hayes, Bruce W., and Rabina Shakya. 2013. "Career Choices and What Influences Nepali Medical Students and Young Doctors: A Cross-Sectional Study." *Human Resources for Health* 11 (1): 5. doi:10.1186/1478-4491-11-5.

Hing, Esther, and Susan M. Schappert. 2012. "Generalist and Specialty Physicians: Supply and Access, 2009–2010." *NCHS Data Brief.*

Huda, Nighat, and Sabira Yousuf. 2006. "Career Preference of Final Year Medical Students of Ziauddin Medical University." *Education for Health: Change in Learning and Practice* 19 (3): 345–53. doi:10.1080/13576280600984087.

Humphries, Niamh, Ruairí Brugha, and Hannah McGee. 2008. "Overseas Nurse Recruitment: Ireland as an Illustration of the Dynamic Nature of Nurse Migration." *Health Policy* 87 (2) (August): 264–72. doi:10.1016/j.healthpol.2007.12.014.

Huntington, Ian, Suvash Shrestha, Nicholas G. Reich, and Amy Hagopian. 2012. "Career Intentions of Medical Students in the Setting of Nepal's Rapidly Expanding Private

Medical Education System." *Health Policy and Planning* 27 (5) (August): 417–28. doi:10.1093/heapol/czr052.

Interprofessional Education Collaborative. 2011. "Core Competencies for Interprofessional Collaborative Practice." Washington, DC.

Jeffe, Donna B., Alison J. Whelan, and Dorothy A. Andriole. 2010. "Primary Care Specialty Choices of United States Medical Graduates, 1997–2006." *Academic Medicine : Journal of the Association of American Medical Colleges* 85 (6): 947–58. doi:10.1097/ACM.0b013e3181dbe77d.

Jiang, H. Joanna, and James W. Begun. 2002. "Dynamics of Change in Local Physician Supply: An Ecological Perspective." *Social Science and Medicine.* doi:10.1016/S0277-9536(01)00132-0.

Jolly, Paul, Clese Erikson, and Gwen Garrison. 2013. "U.S. Graduate Medical Education and Physician Specialty Choice." *Academic Medicine : Journal of the Association of American Medical Colleges* 88 (4) (April): 468–74. doi:10.1097/ACM.0b013e318285199d.

Jones, Robert F., and David Korn. 1997. "On the Cost of Educating a Medical Student." *Academic Medicine : Journal of the Association of American Medical Colleges* 72 (3): 200–10. doi:10.1097/00001888-199703000-00015.

Joseph, N. M., T. Arun Babu, and V. Sharmila. 2010. "Demand-Based Pay: A Distressing Trend in Private Sector Medical Education." *National Medical Journal of India* 23 (6): 375.

Julian, Katherine, Nardine Saad Riegels, and Robert B. Baron. 2011. "Perspective: Creating the Next Generation of General Internists: A Call for Medical Education Reform." *Academic Medicine* 86 (11): 1443–47. doi:10.1097/ACM.0b013e3182303a32.

Kahn, D., S. Pillay, M. G. Veller, E. Panieri, and M. J. R. Westcott. 2006. "General Surgery in Crisis—the Critical Shortage." *South African Journal of Surgery. Suid-Afrikaanse Tydskrif Vir Chirurgie* 44 (3): 88–92, 94.

Kendall-Gallagher, Deborah, Linda H. Aiken, Douglas M. Sloane, and Jeannie P. Cimiotti. 2011. "Nurse Specialty Certification, Inpatient Mortality, and Failure to Rescue." *Journal of Nursing Scholarship* 43 (2) (July): 188–94. doi:10.1111/j.1547-5069.2011.01391.x.

Kerr, Jason R., and Jeffrey J. Brown. 2006. "Costs of a Medical Education: Comparison with Graduate Education in Law and Business." *JACR Journal of the American College of Radiology.* doi:10.1016/j.jacr.2005.09.010.

Khader, Yousef, Dema Al-Zoubi, Zouhair Amarin, Ahmad Alkafagei, Mohammad Khasawneh, Samar Burgan, Khalid El Salem, and Mousa Omari. 2008. "Factors Affecting Medical Students in Formulating Their Specialty Preferences in Jordan." *BMC Medical Education* 8 (32) (January). doi:10.1186/1472-6920-8-32.

Kiolbassa, Kathrin, Antje Miksch, Katja Hermann, Andreas Loh, Joachim Szecsenyi, Stefanie Joos, and Katja Goetz. 2011. "Becoming a General Practitioner—Which Factors Have Most Impact on Career Choice of Medical Students?" *BMC Family Practice* 12 (25). doi:10.1186/1471-2296-12-25.

Kirigia, Joses Muthuri, Akpa Raphael Gbary, Lenity Kainyu Muthuri, Jennifer Nyoni, and Anthony Seddoh. 2006. "The Cost of Health Professionals' Brain Drain in Kenya." *BMC Health Services Research* 6 (89). doi:10.1186/1472-6963-6-89.

Koike, Soichi, Shinya Matsumoto, Tomoko Kodama, Hiroo Ide, Hideo Yasunaga, and Tomoaki Imamura. 2010. "Specialty Choice and Physicians' Career Paths in Japan: An

Analysis of National Physician Survey Data from 1996 to 2006." *Health Policy* 98 (2–3) (December): 236–44. doi:10.1016/j.healthpol.2010.06.021.

Kroneman, Madelon, Pascal Meeus, Dionne Sofia Kringos, Wim Groot, and Jouke van der Zee. 2013. "International Developments in Revenues and Incomes of General Practitioners from 2000 to 2010." *BMC Health Services Research* 13: 436. doi:10.1186/1472–6963–13–436.

Kroneman, Madelon W., Jouke Van der Zee, and Wim Groot. 2009. "Income Development of General Practitioners in Eight European Countries from 1975 to 2005." *BMC Health Services Research* 9: 26. doi:10.1186/1472–6963–9–26.

Kumar, Sanjay. 2004. "Report Highlights Shortcomings in Private Medical Schools in India." *BMJ (Clinical Research Ed.)* 328 (7431) (January 10): 70. doi:10.1136/bmj.328.7431.70–i.

Kwizera, Enoch N., Ehi U. Igumbor, and Lizo E. Mazwai. 2005. "Twenty Years of Medical Education in Rural South Africa—Experiences of the University of Transkei Medical School and Lessons for the Future." *South African Medical Journal = Suid-Afrikaanse Tydskrif Vir Geneeskunde* 95 (12) (December): 920–22, 924.

Lambert, Trevor, and Michael Goldacre. 2011. "Trends in Doctors' Early Career Choices for General Practice in the UK: Longitudinal Questionnaire Surveys." *British Journal of General Practice* 61 (588): e397–403. doi:10.3399/bjgp11X583173.

Lambert, Trevor, Raph Goldacre, Fay Smith, and Michael J. Goldacre. 2012. "Reasons Why Doctors Choose or Reject Careers in General Practice: National Surveys." *British Journal of General Practice* 62 (605): e851–58. doi:10.3399/bjgp12X659330.

Lambert, Trevor W., Michael J. Goldacre, C. Edwards, and J. Parkhouse. 1996. "Career Preferences of Doctors Who Qualified in the United Kingdom in 1993 Compared with Those of Doctors Qualifying in 1974, 1977, 1980, and 1983." *BMJ (Clinical Research Ed.)* 313 (7048): 19–24. doi:10.1136/bmj.313.7048.19.

Lambert, Trevor W., Michael J. Goldacre, and Gill Turner. 2006. "Career Choices of United Kingdom Medical Graduates of 2002: Questionnaire Survey." *Medical Education* 40 (6) (June): 514–21. doi:10.1111/j.1365-2929.2006.02480.x.

Lapolla, Michael, Edward N. Brandt, Andréa Barker, and Lori Ryan. 2004. "The Economic Impacts of Oklahoma's Family Medicine Residency Programs." *The Journal of the Oklahoma State Medical Association* 97 (6) (June): 248–51.

Larson, Margaret Sarfatti. 1977. *The Rise of Professionalism: A Sociological Analysis.* Berkeley, CA: University of California Press.

Lassi, Zohra S., Giorgio Cometto, Luis Huicho, and Zulfiqar A. Bhutta. 2013. "Quality of Care Provided by Mid-Level Health Workers: Systematic Review and Meta-Analysis." *Bulletin of the World Health Organization* 91 (11) (November 1): 824–33I. doi:10.2471/BLT.13.118786.

Laurell, Asa Cristina. 2007. "Health System Reform in Mexico: A Critical Review." *International Journal of Health Services : Planning, Administration, Evaluation* 37 (3): 515–35. doi:10.2190/0133-572V-564N–4831.

Lefevre, Jérémie H., Morgan Roupret, Solen Kerneis, and Laurent Karila. 2010. "Career Choices of Medical Students: A National Survey of 1780 Students." *Medical Education* 44 (6): 603–12. doi:10.1111/j.1365-2923.2010.03707.x.

Leffler, K. B., and C. M. Lindsay. 1981. "Markets for Medical Care and Medical Education: An Integrated Long-Run Structural Approach." *The Journal of Human Resources* 16 (1): 20–40.

Leigh, J. Paul, Daniel Tancredi, Anthony Jerant, Patrick S. Romano, and Richard L. Kravitz. 2012. "Lifetime Earnings for Physicians Across Specialties." *Medical Care* 50 (12) (December): 1. doi:10.1097/MLR.0b013e318268ac0c.

Lind, D. Scott, and Juan C. Cendan. 2003. "Two Decades of Student Career Choice at the University of Florida: Increasingly a Lifestyle Decision." *American Surgeon* 69: 53–55.

Lindley, P. J., L. Sayer, and V. J. Thurtle. 2011. "Current Educational Challenges for Specialist Community Public Health Nurses Following a Health-Visiting Pathway and the Consequences of These Challenges for Public Health." *Perspectives in Public Health* 131 (1): 32–37. doi:10.1177/1757913910369091.

Long, Sharon K. 2008. "On the Road to Universal Coverage: Impacts of Reform in Massachusetts at One Year." *Health Affairs* 27 (4): w270–85. doi:10.1377/hlthaff.27.4.w270.

Long, Sharon K., and Paul B. Masi. 2009. "Access and Affordability: An Update on Health Reform in Massachusetts, Fall 2008." *Health Affairs* 28 (4): w578–87. doi:10.1377/hlthaff.28.4.w578.

Luiz, Ronir Raggio, and Lígia Bahia. 2009. "Income and Vocational Integration of Brazilian Physicians since the Establishment of the National Health System." *Revista de Saude Publica* 43 (4): 689–98.

Mæstad, Ottar, Gaute Torsvik, and Arild Aakvik. 2010. "Overworked? On the Relationship between Workload and Health Worker Performance." *Journal of Health Economics* 29 (5) (September): 686–98. doi:10.1016/j.jhealeco.2010.05.006.

Mahal, Ajay, and Manoj Mohanan. 2006. "Growth of Private Medical Education in India." *Medical Education* 40 (10) (October): 1009–11. doi:10.1111/j.1365-2929.2006.02560.x.

Mahal, Ajay S., and Naseem Shah. 2006. "Implications of the Growth of Dental Education in India." *Journal of Dental Education* 70 (8): 884–91.

Malvárez, Silvina, Christianne Famer Rocha, María Cristina Cometo, and Patricia Fabiana Gomez. 2008. "Serie 55: Notas Preliminares Sobre Migración Y Escasez de Enfermeras En América Latina." Washington, DC.

Mariolis, Anargiros, Constantinos Mihas, Alevizos Alevizos, Vasilis Gizlis, Theodoros Mariolis, Konstantinos Marayiannis, Yiannis Tountas, Christodoulos Stefanadis, Anastas Philalithis, and George Creatsas. 2007. "General Practice as a Career Choice among Undergraduate Medical Students in Greece." *BMC Medical Education* 7: 15. doi:10.1186/1472-6920-7-15.

Marschall, Jeff G., and Ahmer A. Karimuddin. 2003. "Decline in Popularity of General Surgery as a Career Choice in North America: Review of Postgraduate Residency Training Selection in Canada, 1996–2001." *World Journal of Surgery.* doi:10.1007/s00268-002-6642-48.

Matsumoto, Masatoshi, Kazuo Inoue, Robert Bowman, and Eiji Kajii. 2010. "Self-Employment, Specialty Choice, and Geographical Distribution of Physicians in Japan: A Comparison with the United States." *Health Policy* 96 (3): 239–44. doi:10.1016/j.healthpol.2010.02.008.

Mbindyo, Patrick, Duane Blaauw, and Mike English. 2013. "The Role of Clinical Officers in the Kenyan Health System: A Question of Perspective." *Human Resources for Health* 11 (1) (January): 32. doi:10.1186/1478-4491-11-32.

McEldowney, Rene P., and Arnold Berry. 1995. "Physician Supply and Distribution in the USA." *Journal of Management in Medicine* 9 (5): 68–74. doi:10.1108/02689239510096839.

McManus, I. C. 2005. "The Wealth of Distinguished Doctors: Retrospective Survey." *BMJ (Clinical Research Ed.)* 331 (7531) (December 24): 1520–23. doi:10.1136/bmj.331.7531.1520.

McPake, Barbara, Akiko Maeda, Edson Correia Araújo, Christophe Lemiere, Atef El Maghraby, and Giorgio Cometto. 2013. "Why Do Health Labour Market Forces Matter?" *Bulletin of the World Health Organization* 91 (11) (December 1): 841–46. doi:10.2471/BLT.13.118794.

McPake, Barbara, Scott Anthony, and Ijeoma Edoka. 2014. *Analyzing Markets for Health Workers: Insights from Labor and Health Economics.* Washington, DC: World Bank. doi:10.1596/978-1-4648-0224-9.

McWilliams, Brent Robert, Bonnie Schmidt, and Michael R. Bleich. 2013. "Men in Nursing." *American Journal of Nursing* 113 (1): 38–44.

Medhanyie, Araya, Mark Spigt, Yohannes Kifle, Nikki Schaay, David Sanders, Roman Blanco, Dinant GeertJan, and Yemane Berhane. 2012. "The Role of Health Extension Workers in Improving Utilization of Maternal Health Services in Rural Areas in Ethiopia: A Cross Sectional Study." *BMC Health Services Research* 12 (1): 352. doi:10.1186/1472-6963-12-352.

Mills, Edward J., Steve Kanters, Amy Hagopian, Nick Bansback, Jean Nachega, Mark Alberton, Christopher G. Au-Yeung, Andy Mtambo, Ivy L. Bourgeault, Samuel Luboga, Robert S. Hogg, and Nathan Ford. 2011. "The Financial Cost of Doctors Emigrating from Sub-Saharan Africa: Human Capital Analysis." *BMJ* 343: d7031. doi:10.1136/bmj.d7031.

Moore, James, Jesse Gale, Kevin Dew, and Don Simmers. 2006. "Student Debt amongst Junior Doctors in New Zealand; Part 2: Effects on Intentions and Workforce." *New Zealand Medical Journal* 119 (1229): 21–28.

Mullan, Fitzhugh, Candice Chen, Stephen Petterson, Gretchen Kolsky, and Michael Spagnola. 2010. "The Social Mission of Medical Education: Ranking the Schools." *Annals of Internal Medicine* 152 (12): 804–11. doi:10.1016/j.yped.2010.12.009.

Mullan, Fitzhugh, Seble Frehywot, Francis Omaswa, Eric Buch, Candice Chen, S. Ryan Greysen, Travis Wassermann, Seble Frehywot, Francis Omaswa, Eric Buch, Candice Chen, S Ryan Greysen, Travis Wassermann, Diaa ElDin ElGaili Abubakr, Magda Awases, Charles Boelen, Mohenou Jean-Marie Isidore Diomande, Delanyo Dovlo, Josefo Ferro, Abraham Haileamlak, Jehu Iputo, Marian Jacobs, Abdel Karim Koumaré, Mwapatsa Mipando, Gottleib Lobe Monekosso, Emiola Oluwabunmi Olapade-Olaopa, Paschalis Rugarabamu, Nelson K Sewankambo, Heather Ross, Huda Ayas, Selam Bedada Chale, Soeurette Cyprien, Jordan Cohen, Tenagne Haile-Mariam, Ellen Hamburger, Laura Jolley, Joseph C Kolars, Gilbert Kombe, and Andre-Jacques Neusy,. 2011. "Medical Schools in Sub-Saharan Africa." *The Lancet* 377 (9771): 1113–21. doi:10.1016/S0140-6736(10)61961-7.

Nagral, Sanjay. 2010. "Ketan Desai and the Medical Council of India: The Road to Perdition?" *Indian Journal of Medical Ethics* VII (3; July–September): 134–5.

Namate, Dorothy E. 1995. "The Cost of Registered Nurse-Midwifery Education in Malawi." *Journal of Advanced Nursing* 22 (3):410–15.doi:10.1046/j.1365-2648.1995.22030410.x.

Nair, Manisha, and Premila Webster. 2010. "Education for Health Professionals in the Emerging Market Economies: A Literature Review." Medical Education 44: 856–63. doi:10.1111/j.1365-2923.2010.03747.x.

Nash, Kent D., and L. Jackson Brown. 2012. "The Structure and Economics of Dental Education." *Journal of Dental Education* 76 (8) (August 1): 987–95.

Nash, Kent D., and David L. Pfeifer. 2006. "Prosthodontics as a Specialty Private Practice: Net Income of Private Practitioners." *Journal of Prosthodontics* 15 (1): 37–46. doi:10.1111/j.1532-849X.2006.00067.x.

Newbold, David. 2008. "The Production Economics of Nursing: A Discussion Paper." *International Journal of Nursing Studies* 45 (1): 120–28. doi:10.1016/j.ijnurstu.2007.01.007.

Newton, Dale A., Martha S. Grayson, and Lori Foster Thompson. 2005. "The Variable Influence of Lifestyle and Income on Medical Students' Career Specialty Choices: Data from Two U.S. Medical Schools, 1998–2004." *Academic Medicine : Journal of the Association of American Medical Colleges* 80 (9): 809–14. doi:10.1097/00001888-200509000-00005.

Nigenda, Gustavo, and Maria Helena Machado. 2000. "From State to Market: The Nicaraguan Labour Market for Health Personnel." *Health Policy and Planning* 15 (3): 312–18. doi:10.1093/heapol/15.3.312.

Nigenda, Gustavo H., José Arturo Ruiz, and Rosa Bejarano. 2005. "Educational and Labor Wastage of Doctors in Mexico: Towards the Construction of a Common Methodology." *Human Resources for Health* 3 (1) (April 15): 3. doi:10.1186/1478-4491-3-3.

Pan, S., and L. Straub. 1997. "Returns to Nursing Education: Rural and Nonrural Practice." *The Journal of Rural Health : Official Journal of the American Rural Health Association and the National Rural Health Care Association* 13 (1) (January): 78–85. doi:10.1111/j.1748-0361.1997.tb00836.x.

Parfitt, Barbara. 2009. "Health Reform: The Human Resource Challenges for Central Asian Commonwealth of Independent States (CIS) Countries." *Collegian* 16 (1): 35–40. doi:10.1016/j.colegn.2009.01.002.

Perales, Francisco. 2013. "Occupational Sex-Segregation, Specialized Human Capital and Wages: Evidence from Britain." *Work, Employment & Society* 27 (4) (May): 600–20. doi:10.1177/0950017012460305.

Pikoulis, Emmanouil, Efthimios D. Avgerinos, Xanthi Pedeli, Ioannis Karavokyros, Neofitos Bassios, and Sofia Anagnostopoulou. 2010. "Medical Students' Perceptions on Factors Influencing a Surgical Career: The Fate of General Surgery in Greece." *Surgery* 148 (3): 510–15. doi:10.1016/j.surg.2010.01.013.

Preston, Barbara. 2009. "The Australian Nurse and Midwifery Workforce: Issues, Developments and the Future." *Collegian* 16 (1): 25–34. doi:10.1016/j.colegn.2008.12.002.

Rao, Krishna D., T. Sundararaman, Aarushi Bhatnagar, Garima Gupta, Puni Kokho, and Kamlesh Jain. 2013. "Which Doctor for Primary Health Care? Quality of Care and Non-Physician Clinicians in India." *Social Science and Medicine* 84 (May): 30–34. doi:10.1016/j.socscimed.2013.02.018.

Reschovsky, James D., and Andrea B. Staiti. 2005. "Physician Incomes in Rural and Urban America." *Issue Brief (Center for Studying Health System Change)*.

Reynolds, Jaratdao, Thunthita Wisaijohn, Nareerut Pudpong, Nantiya Watthayu, Alex Dalliston, Rapeepong Suphanchaimat, Weerasak Putthasri, and Krisada Sawaengdee. 2013. "A Literature Review: The Role of the Private Sector in the Production of

Nurses in India, Kenya, South Africa and Thailand." *Human Resources for Health* 11 (1) (January): 14. doi:10.1186/1478-4491-11-14.

Richards, L., B. Symon, D. Burrow, A. Chartier, G. Misan, and D. Wilkinson. 2002. "Undergraduate Student Experience in Dental Service Delivery in Rural South Australia: An Analysis of Costs and Benefits." *Australian Dental Journal* 47 (3): 254–58.

Riley, Patricia L., Alexandra Zuber, Stephen M. Vindigni, Neeru Gupta, Andre R. Verani, Nadine L. Sunderland, Michael Friedman, P. Zurn, C. Okoro, H. Patrick, and J. Campbell.. 2012. "Information Systems on Human Resources for Health: A Global Review." *Human Resources for Health* 10: 7. doi:10.1186/1478-4491-10-7.

Robinson, Sarah, Trevor Murrells, and Peter Griffiths. 2008. "Investigating the Dynamics of Nurse Migration in Early Career: A Longitudinal Questionnaire Survey of Variation in Regional Retention of Diploma Qualifiers in England." *International Journal of Nursing Studies* 45 (7): 1064–80. doi:10.1016/j.ijnurstu.2007.07.001.

Rohlfing, James, Ryan Navarro, Omar Z. Maniya, Byron D. Hughes, and Derek K. Rogalsky. 2014. "Medical Student Debt and Major Life Choices Other than Specialty." *Medical Education Online* 19 (25603). doi:10.3402/meo.v19.25603.

Sana, Mariano. 2008. "Growth of Migrant Remittances from the United States to Mexico, 1990-2004." *Social Forces* 86 (3): 995–1025. doi:10.2307/20430785.

Schroeder, Steven A. 1993. "Training an Appropriate Mix of Physicians to Meet the Nation's Needs." *Academic Medicine : Journal of the Association of American Medical Colleges* 68 (2): 118–22. doi:10.1097/00001888-199302000-00002.

Schumacher, Edward J. 2002. "Technology, Skills, and Health Care Labor Markets." *Journal of Labor Research* 23 (3) (September): 397–415.

Schwartz, Mark D., William T. Basco, Michael R. Grey, Joann G. Elmore, and Arthur Rubenstein. 2005. "Rekindling Student Interest in Generalist Careers." *Annals of Internal Medicine* 142 (8): 715–24.

Scott, Ian, Bruce Wright, Fraser Brenneis, Pamela Brett-MacLean, and Laurie McCaffrey. 2007. "Why Would I Choose a Career in Family Medicine? Reflections of Medical Students at 3 Universities." *Canadian Family Physician* 53 (11): 1956–57.

Selva, Olid Anna, Amando Martin Zurro, Josep Jimenez Villa, Xavier Mundet Tuduri, Antonio Monreal Hijar, Angel Otero Puime, Gemma Mas Dalmau, and Pablo Alonso Coello. 2012. "Medical Students' Perceptions and Attitudes about Family Practice: A Qualitative Research Synthesis." *BMC Medical Education* 12 (1): 81. doi:10.1186/1472-6920-12-81.

Shankar, P. Ravi, and Trilok P. Thapa. 2010. "Applying the Concept of 'Field' to Private Medical Schools in Nepal." *Medical Education*. doi:10.1111/j.1365-2923.2010.03805.x.

Shehnaz, Syed Ilyas. 2011. "Privatization of Medical Education in Asia." *South-East Asian Journal of Medical Education* 5 (2): 18–25.

Shipman, Scott A., Karen C. Jones, Clese E. Erikson, and Shana F. Sandberg. 2013. "Exploring the Workforce Implications of a Decade of Medical School Expansion: Variations in Medical School Growth and Changes in Student Characteristics and Career Plans." *Academic Medicine : Journal of the Association of American Medical Colleges* 88 (12) (December): 1904–12. doi:10.1097/ACM.0000000000000040.

Simon, Carol J., David Dranove, and William D. White. 1998. "The Effect of Managed Care on the Incomes of Primary Care and Specialty Physicians." *Health Services Research* 33 (3 Pt 1): 549–69.

Siribaddana, Nipuna, Suneth Agampodi, and Sisira Siribaddana. 2012. "Private Medical Education in Sri Lanka." *Indian Journal of Medical Ethics* 9 (4): 269–71.

Sochalski, Julie, and Johnathan Weiner. 2011. "Appendix F: Health Care System Reform and the Nursing Workforce: Matching Nursing Practice and Skills to Furture Needs, Not Past Demands." In *The Future of Nursing: Leading Change, Advancing Health*, 375–03. Washington, DC: The National Academies Press.

Spetz, Joanne, and Timothy Bates. 2013. "Is a Baccalaureate in Nursing Worth It? The Return to Education, 2000–2008." *Health Services Research* 48 (6 PART1) (December): 1859–78. doi:10.1111/1475–6773.12104.

Stanback, John, Anthony K. Mbonye, and Martha Bekiita. 2007. "Contraceptive Injections by Community Health Workers in Uganda: A Nonrandomized Community Trial." *Bulletin of the World Health Organization* 85 (10) (October): 768–73. doi:10.2471/BLT.07.040162.

Stange, Kevin. 2014. "How Does Provider Supply and Regulation Influence Health Care Markets? Evidence from Nurse Practitioners and Physician Assistant." *Journal of Health Economics* 33: 1–27.

Starfield, Barbara, Leiyu Shi, Atul Grover, and James Macinko. 2005. "The Effects of Specialist Supply on Populations' Health: Assessing the Evidence." *Health Affairs (Project Hope)* Suppl Web: 97–107. doi:10.1377/hlthaff.w5.97.

Starfield, Barbara, Leiyu Shi, and James Macinko. 2005. "Contribution of Primary Care to Health Systems and Health." *Milbank Quarterly*. doi:10.1111/j.1468-0009.2005.00409.x.

Vanasse, Alain, Maria Gabriela Orzanco, Josiane Courteau, and Sarah Scott. 2011. "Attractiveness of Family Medicine for Medical Students: Influence of Research and Debt." *Canadian Family Physician* 57 (6): e216–27.

Van Ginneken, Nadja, Prathap Tharyan, Simon Lewin, Girish N. Rao, Renee Romeo, and Vikram Patel. 2011. "Non-Specialist Health Worker Interventions for Mental Health Care in Low- and Middle- Income Countries." *The Cochrane Database of Systematic Reviews* 2011 (5) (May 11). doi:10.1002/14651858.CD009149.

Walker, Damian, Jeanne M. McDermott, Julia Fox-Rushby, Marwan Tanjung, Mardiati Nadjib, Dono Widiatmoko, and Endang Achadi. 2002. "An Economic Analysis of Midwifery Training Programmes in South Kalimantan, Indonesia." *Bulletin of the World Health Organization* 80 (1): 47–55. doi:S0042-96862002000100009 [pii].

Walker, Dilys, Lisa M. Demaria, Leticia Suarez, and Leslie Cragin. 2012. "Skilled Birth Attendants in Mexico: How Does Care During Normal Birth by General Physicians, Obstetric Nurses, and Professional Midwives Compare with World Health Organization Evidence-Based Practice Guidelines?" *Journal of Midwifery and Women's Health* 57 (1): 18–27. doi:10.1111/j.1542-2011.2011.00075.x.

Weeks, William B., and Amy E. Wallace. 2002a. "Medicare Payment Changes and Physicians' Incomes." *Journal of Health Care Finance* 29 (2) (January): 18–26.

———. 2002b. "The More Things Change: Revisiting a Comparison of Educational Costs and Incomes of Physicians and Other Professionals." *Academic Medicine : Journal of the Association of American Medical Colleges* 77 (4) (April): 312–19.

——. 2002c. "Long-Term Financial Implications of Specialty Training for Physicians." *The American Journal of Medicine* 113 (5) (October 1): 393–99.

——. 2003. "Time and Money: A Retrospective Evaluation of the Inputs, Outputs, Efficiency, and Incomes of Physicians." *Archives of Internal Medicine* 163 (8) (April 28): 944–48. doi:10.1001/archinte.163.8.944.

Weeks, William B., Amy E. Wallace, Myron M. Wallace, and H. Gilbert Welch. 1994. "A Comparison of the Educational Costs and Incomes of Physicians and Other Professionals." *The New England Journal of Medicine* 330 (18) (May 5): 1280–86. doi:10.1097/00132586–199412000–00060.

Weeks, William B., and Tanner A. Wallace. 2008. "Medical School Type and Physician Income." *Journal of Health Care Finance* 34 (3) (January): 34–44.

Weissman, Charles, Rachel Yaffa Zisk-Rony, Josh E. Schroeder, Yoram G. Weiss, Alex Avidan, Uriel Elchalal, and Howard Tandeter. 2012. "Medical Specialty Considerations by Medical Students Early in Their Clinical Experience." *Israel Journal of Health Policy Research* 1 (1): 13. doi:10.1186/2045–4015–1–13.

Wilder, Venis, Martey S. Dodoo, Robert L. Phillips, Bridget Teevan, Andrew W. Bazemore, Stephen M. Petterson, and Imam Xierali. 2010. "Income Disparities Shape Medical Student Specialty Choice." *American Family Physician* 82 (6) (September 15): 601.

Woloschuk, Wayne, Bruce Wright, and Kevin McLaughlin. 2011. "Debiasing the Hidden Curriculum: Academic Equality among Medical Specialties." *Canadian Family Physician* 57 (1): e26–30.

World Health Organization. 2006. "Working Together for Health: The World Health Report 2006." Geneva.

Yathish, T. R., and C. G. Manjula. 2010. "How to Strengthen and Reform Indian Medical Education System: Is Nationalization the Only Answer?" *Online Journal of Health and Allied Sciences* (April 30).

Zárate Hoyos, Germán A. 2008. "International Labor Migration as a Strategy of Economic Stabilization at the Household Level in Mexico and Central America." *Papeles de Poblacion* 56: 19–36.

Environmental Benefits Statement

green
press
INITIATIVE

www.ingramcontent.com/pod-product-compliance
Lightning Source LLC
Chambersburg PA
CBHW081511200326